Cambridge Elements

Elements in Language Teaching
edited by
Heath Rose
Linacre College, University of Oxford
Jim McKinley
University College London

TEACHING YOUNG MULTILINGUAL LEARNERS

Key Issues and New Insights

Luciana C. de Oliveira
Virginia Commonwealth University

Loren Jones
University of Maryland, College Park

CAMBRIDGE
UNIVERSITY PRESS

Shaftesbury Road, Cambridge CB2 8EA, United Kingdom

One Liberty Plaza, 20th Floor, New York, NY 10006, USA

477 Williamstown Road, Port Melbourne, VIC 3207, Australia

314–321, 3rd Floor, Plot 3, Splendor Forum, Jasola District Centre,
New Delhi – 110025, India

103 Penang Road, #05–06/07, Visioncrest Commercial, Singapore 238467

Cambridge University Press is part of Cambridge University Press & Assessment,
a department of the University of Cambridge.

We share the University's mission to contribute to society through the pursuit of
education, learning and research at the highest international levels of excellence.

www.cambridge.org
Information on this title: www.cambridge.org/9781108928809

DOI: 10.1017/9781108934138

First published 2023

A catalogue record for this publication is available from the British Library.

ISBN 978-1-108-92880-9 Paperback
ISSN 2632-4415 (online)
ISSN 2632-4407 (print)

Teaching Young Multilingual Learners

Key Issues and New Insights

Elements in Language Teaching

DOI: 10.1017/9781108934138
First published online: January 2023

Luciana C. de Oliveira
Virginia Commonwealth University

Loren Jones
University of Maryland, College Park

Author for correspondence: Luciana C. de Oliveira, deoliveiral@vcu.edu

Abstract: This Element provides an overview of research focusing on language teaching practices for young multilingual learners in primary classrooms in English-speaking contexts. The term "young multilingual learner" refers to primary school children, with ages ranging from approximately five to twelve years old at various English language proficiency levels. Pedagogy-informed research studies conducted in K-5 classrooms are used to develop research-informed pedagogies for young multilingual learners in primary classrooms. The authors use the notion of culturally sustaining teaching practices to provide examples from pedagogy-informed research studies. The focus on early (K-3) and intermediate (4–5) grades provides a range of illustrations of such practices. The Element concludes with implications for teacher education and the preparation of teachers of young multilingual learners.

Keywords: young multilingual learners, bilingual students, culturally sustaining pedagogies, primary classrooms, English learners

ISBNs: 9781108928809 (PB), 9781108934138 (OC)
ISSNs: 2632-4415 (online), 2632-4407 (print)

Contents

1 Key Concepts in Teaching Young Multilingual Learners

Multilingual learners (ML), students who speak languages other than English, have been an increasing population all over the world for several years (de Oliveira & Westerlund, 2020; Gibbons, 2015; Gunderson, 2009). In Australia, 15 percent of the primary and secondary school student population is students classified as English Learners (ELs) (Michell, 2021). In Canada, over two million students were enrolled in second language programs in 2020 out of a total population of five million primary and secondary students. An increase in the population of students whose first language is not English has also been consistent in the United Kingdom, with 19.3 percent of the primary and secondary school population representing students whose first language is not English in 2021, an increase of 2 percent from 2015 (Clark, 2022). In the United States, more than 9 percent of the US elementary and secondary (K-12) student population consists of students identified as ELs, which represents over 3.8 million students in US schools, as of fall 2020 (NCES, 2020). The largest number of these students is found in California, Florida, Illinois, New Mexico, New York, Puerto Rico, and Texas. However, states such as Arkansas, Alabama, Colorado, Delaware, Georgia, Indiana, Kentucky, Nebraska, North Carolina, South Carolina, Tennessee, Vermont, and Virginia have experienced more than 200 percent growth in the numbers of ELs in schools.

This population growth in many English-speaking countries around the world means that there needs to be a concerted effort to address their needs and prepare their teachers. Typically, these MLs take English as a second language (ESL) classes or participate in programs where both their home language and English are used to develop their language proficiency before they enter the general education classroom. Yet the number of ESL specialists in schools is limited, and many school districts do not serve the full number of these students. Most MLs spend only a portion of their day with bilingual or ESL teachers. These students, then, attend general education classes most of their time in school.

This Element addresses this specific population of students and adds to the existing literature on teacher preparation for MLs in primary English-speaking contexts. We provide an overview of research focusing on language teaching practices for young multilingual learners in primary classrooms. The term "young multilingual learner" refers to primary school children, with ages ranging from approximately five to twelve years old, at various English-language proficiency levels. Pedagogy-informed research studies conducted in primary (K-5) classrooms are used to develop research-informed pedagogies for young multilingual learners in primary classrooms. We use the notion of culturally sustaining teaching practices to provide examples from pedagogy-informed research studies. The focus on early (K-3) and intermediate (4–5) grades provides a range of illustrations of such practices. We conclude with implications for teacher education and the preparation of teachers of young multilingual learners.

1.1 Terminology

The terminology used to describe the target student population we address in this Element varies considerably. There is little agreement in the scholarly literature as to what name best describes these students. Although each designation has different connotations and issues, various terms are favored by researchers within distinct research traditions depending upon one's philosophical commitment, sociopolitical orientation, and unique focus. These include emergent to advanced bilingual student (EAB), multilingual learner (ML), bi/multilingual student, plurilingual learner, additional language speaker, English language learner (ELL), English learner (EL), limited English proficient (LEP) student, non-native speaker (NNS), second language (L2) speaker, among others. We chose to use the term "multilingual learner" (ML) in this Element since it has a positive connotation that emphasizes these students' various language abilities, instead of using other terms highlighting the students' limitations (e.g., LEP and NNS) or with a focus on English learning (e.g., ELL and EL). The term "MLs" refers to students who speak a language or languages other than English at home and who are learning English as an additional language. Young multilingual learners are children in primary schools, with ages ranging from approximately five to twelve years old at various English language proficiency levels. This intentional designation aims to underscore the linguistic assets that MLs bring to the classroom (García & Kleyn, 2016).

1.2 Teacher Preparation for Multilingual Learners

General education teachers who did not have this student population before in their classes are now seeing high numbers of MLs among their students. General education, content area teachers need knowledge and practical ideas about addressing the academic language needs of MLs because they have the dual responsibility of facilitating MLs' content learning while also supporting their ongoing English language development. Teachers need to develop a knowledge base, expertise, and competencies necessary to effectively work with MLs. There is evidence that many in-service and pre-service teachers feel uncomfortable and unprepared to work with MLs, and need theoretical and experiential knowledge about Second Language Acquisition (SLA), English language development, and teaching MLs (Peercy et al., 2022).

This needed preparation includes specific competencies – essential skills, knowledge, and dispositions – that all teachers should develop for teaching MLs (Faltis, Arias, & Ramírez-Marín, 2010; Howard & Aleman, 2008). These include subject matter and pedagogical knowledge, integration of pedagogy, learning and culture; knowledge of effective practices that include understanding of students' lives, communities, and larger social and political discourses; understanding the distinction between everyday and academic language; knowledge of SLA; understanding the role of home language (L1) in learning the second language (L2); advocating for MLs; drawing on community engagement; and using multiple assessments. Another area that has been deemed effective in teaching MLs is the ability to tap into different "funds of knowledge" (Moll et al., 1992) that students' families share. Moll's research addressed how family members use their funds of knowledge to sustain their families both economically and socially, and how these relationships connect them with other members of the community.

Guided by a socially oriented theory of language, which places special importance on the relationship between contexts and patterns of language choices for meaning making, teachers can provide opportunities to prepare language learners to participate in authentic learning contexts and meaning making through scaffolding (Hammond & Gibbons, 2005). Classrooms where teachers are able to create an environment with high challenge and high support are those where not only MLs but all students can benefit (Hammond & Gibbons, 2005).

Knowing how to support MLs' academic language development continues to be a key competency for teachers (Cummins 2001; Peercy et al., 2022; Schleppegrell 2004). Recent criticism targeting the teaching and learning of academic language has labeled them as hegemonic (Flores & Rosa, 2015). This perspective claims that instruction focused on academic language idealizes the linguistic practices of White people and devalues minoritized speakers' linguistic repertoires (Flores & Rosa, 2015; García, 2020). But scholars in various fields have refuted these claims. They show how pedagogical approaches that focus on the development of academic language value and draw on minoritized speakers' languaging practices while enabling their access to discourse practices typical of schooling (e.g., Cummins, 2001; Harman & Khote, 2018; Schleppegrell, 2020). Some have called for the characterization of academic language as a hybrid that includes everyday and disciplinary ways of knowing (Gutiérrez et al., 2010). Teachers of young MLs can draw on the cultures of students, connect to their backgrounds and experiences, and use students' home languages and linguistic repertoires at the same time as they are *code-breaking*, or addressing the academic language demands of various content areas (de Oliveira, 2016; de Oliveira, Jones, & Smith, 2020). Students' cultural and language affordances are optimized as joint learning activities with the development of academic language. This requires effective support, including support in what Gibbons (2015) calls "literate talk," or talk that introduces concepts and provides discipline-specific ways of talking about these concepts with students. This kind of support that MLs need to receive starts in kindergarten, with the teacher using specific ways to scaffold language and learning (Gibbons 2014); therefore, teachers working with MLs need to have a deep understanding of these constructs in order to be effective with these students.

The purposeful use of the first language in the second language classroom is another key competency. However, monolingual instructional assumptions permeate second language education. Cummins (2005) highlights the following premises as the most common: "instruction should be carried out exclusively in the target language, without recourse to L1," "translation between L1 and L2 has no place in the learning and teaching of literacy," "in L2 immersion and bilingual programs, the two languages should be kept separate" (p. 588). More so, in many classrooms, students' heritage language is considered an impediment or is irrelevant to learning English (Cummins, 2005). Monolingual teaching approaches fundamentally disregard the nature of learning a new language, a process in which learners always relate the new language to the language they already know, whether they are consciously or unconsciously doing it. This is in spite of a substantial body of scholarship demonstrating that instructional programs, teaching strategies and educational policies, lesson objectives and tasks can and should integrate students' languages and cultures (García & Jensen 2009; García & Li, 2014). Utilizing students' L1 in the classroom has been proposed as a pedagogy that offers very positive results to oppose monolingual assumptions among teachers.

1.3 Teaching Young Multilingual Learners

Research on teaching young multilingual learners has shown that there are specific benefits for early language development in English, including increased time spent on language development, pronunciation and fluency facility, greater global awareness and intercultural knowledge, and development of bilingualism (Shin & Crandall, 2013). Other specific relevant content identified in the literature includes authentic language learning experiences (Short et al., 2018), culturally relevant texts (Herrera et al., 2015), scaffolding (Hammond & Gibbons, 2005), message abundancy (Gibbons, 2015), and collaborative work with peers (de Oliveira, 2016). These practices are all relevant for addressing MLs' cultural, linguistic, and overall academic needs (Hite & Evans, 2006).

Given the amount of time that young MLs spend with teachers, teacher discourse plays a significant role in their education, with the nature of these interactions having a major impact on student success (e.g., Johnson, 2019). As the medium of instruction, teachers' language is directly connected to the content students learn. Moreover, teacher discourse models different registers, exposing students to academic language across subject areas and influencing how students view learning, language, themselves, and even their surrounding world (Johnston, 2012). Because of the critical importance of teacher discourse for young MLs' language development, this Element highlights several excerpts and lessons focused on language from early (K-3) and intermediate (4–5) grades.

We organized this Element into three sections:

- **Practices for Teaching Young Multilingual Learners**, where we review research focusing on language teaching practices for young multilingual learners in primary classrooms. We emphasize contexts where English is the dominant language and medium of instruction.
- **Practices in Action: Evidence and Examples from Pedagogy-Informed Research Studies**, where we provide five main practices and specific examples from our classroom-based research in grades K-5 to illustrate a range of culturally sustaining teaching practices. We define pedagogy-informed research as connected to classrooms that specifically address pedagogical practices for MLs in the context of a general education classroom.
- **Implications for Teacher Education**, where we conclude the Element with implications for teacher education and the preparation of teachers of young multilingual learners.

2 Practices for Teaching Young Multilingual Learners

This section reviews research focusing on language teaching practices for young multilingual learners in primary classrooms. We emphasize contexts where English is the dominant language and medium of instruction.

2.1 Culturally Sustaining Pedagogies

Culturally sustaining pedagogies (Paris & Alim, 2012) build on the ever-popular concept of culturally responsive teaching (Ladson-Billings, 2014) by going beyond the act of making content relevant to students and responding to their cultures, which Paris (2012) has stated does not necessarily help "sustain and support bi- and multilingualism and bi- and multiculturalism" (p. 95). Instead, culturally sustaining pedagogies address the multiethnic and multilingual nature of many classrooms and help support "the cultural and linguistic competence of their communities while simultaneously offering access to dominant cultural competence" (p. 95). Paris advocates for a pedagogy that maintains the practices of students while also expanding their repertoires to include "dominant language[s], literacies and other cultural practices" (p. 95) so students are also able to critique such practices. Importantly, one of the goals of culturally sustaining pedagogies is to help perpetuate and foster "linguistic, literate, and cultural pluralism as part of the democratic project of schooling" (Paris, 2012, p. 95) which is a crucial goal in the education of multilingual learners. Paris and Alim (2012) suggest that, "culturally sustaining pedagogy exists wherever education sustains the lifeways of communities who have been and continue to be damaged and erased through schooling" (p. 1).

   With such rich multiethnic and multilingual classrooms in various parts of the world, we find it essential to highlight specific instructional practices that embody culturally sustaining pedagogies that enable educators to create learning environments in which all students are educated effectively and equitably.

2.2 Enacting Culturally Sustaining Pedagogies

There are a number of language teaching practices identified in the literature as effective strategies for working with young multilingual learners, but for our purposes we highlight those that we believe enact culturally sustaining pedagogies for young multilingual learners in primary classrooms: incorporating students' funds of knowledge, drawing on interactional scaffolding moves, utilizing students' L1, using multimodal instruction, and applying a functional approach to language development (see Figure 1).

2.2.1 Incorporating Students' Funds of Knowledge

One practice that enacts culturally sustaining pedagogies is incorporating students' funds of knowledge (FOK; Moll et al., 1992) in the classroom. The term "FOK," initially defined as "historically accumulated and culturally developed bodies of knowledge and skills essential for household or individual functioning and well-being" (Moll et al., 1992, p. 133), has evolved to now include students' interests more broadly (Hedges et al., 2011) and the ways of knowing that they develop from peer groups, communities, and popular culture (Moje et al., 2004). As such, we define students' FOK as the dynamic knowledge, skills, and practices developed in households and

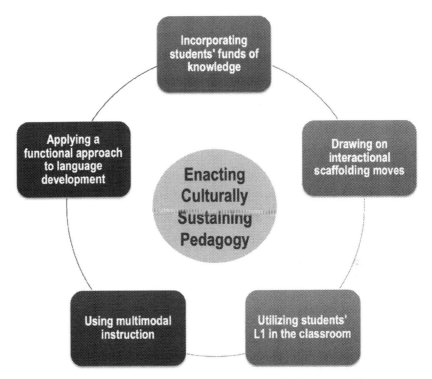

Figure 1 Practices to enact culturally sustaining pedagogies

communities (de Jong et al., 2013; Moje et al., 2004; Moll et al., 1992). Students' FOK are crucial sources of information that can lead to more effective teaching practices (Hogg, 2011), but it takes purposeful planning that can be challenging, especially when teachers are faced with scripted curricula (Mead, 2021).

Researchers have long advocated for curriculum and instruction to draw on students' FOK (see Hogg, 2011; Llopart & Esteban-Guitart, 2018; Rodriguez, 2013; Short et al., 2018) and prior research has examined how teachers leverage students' FOK in the classroom in order to create a more inclusive, engaging learning environment, to support students in understanding new content, and to assist students in developing their English language skills (e.g., Blair et al., 2018; Keefer et al., 2020). For example, Turner and others (2019) leveraged elementary students' experiences and understandings as they were introduced to mathematical modeling. More specifically, students drew on their prior experiences to identify important quantities and relationships, to make assumptions, to analyze and interpret the reasonableness of their solutions, and to revise their models when needed.

2.2.2 Drawing on Interactional Scaffolding Moves

Another practice that enacts culturally sustaining pedagogy is utilizing inter-actional scaffolding in the classroom. Early scholars in the field (e.g., Wood et al., 1976) recognized that scaffolding was a means for adults to help children work within their zone of proximal development (ZPD; Vygotsky, 1978), effectively bridging the gap between their current and future independent performance. This scaffolding is often accomplished as students work with a teacher or a more advanced peer, gradually releasing responsibility as they become capable of successfully completing the assigned task on their own (Bruner, 1983).

While scaffolding originated in studies of tutoring (e.g., Wood et al., 1976), it has since evolved to capture classroom research and practice (e.g., Athanases & de Oliveira, 2014), where it has shown to be especially important for MLs' participation in classroom discourse (Hammond & Gibbons, 2005). Interactional scaffolding involves teachers making use of different moves, making explicit connections between students' prior experiences and their current and future learning, using appropriation, recasting, elaboration, cued elicitation, and recapping. These moves are instrumental in how teachers engage students in the learning environment, and they can support multilingual learners in developing oral language in the context of the classroom along with skills for interacting in a range of situations. Participation in rich classroom discourse is a key resource for learning from elementary to middle school years and beyond, where the language of schooling becomes more demanding (Gibbons, 2006; Schleppegrell, 2004).

Classroom discourse, and specifically the notion of interactional scaffolding, appears to be a promising practice in classrooms with MLs (Garton & Copland, 2019; Hammond & Gibbons, 2005; Johnson, 2019; Short et al., 2018). Typically, this scaffolding is implemented through the initiation, response, and feedback sequence (IRF). Teachers implement the IRF sequence by asking a question, listening thoughtfully to students' responses, and providing feedback in a way that encourages students to remain engaged, at times by asking them to clarify their response, provide additional details, or ask a question of their own. The IRF sequence contrasts with the typical structure of classroom discourse, Initiation-Response-Evaluation (IRE), which has been shown to inhibit continued conversation (Mehan, 1979). Based on the context, teachers can draw on any one of the various scaffolding moves when providing feedback to students. For instance, the teacher may incorporate students' prior knowledge and experiences, referencing their unique out-of-school and home experiences and shared experiences from previous teaching and learning activities. The teacher might also utilize cued elicitation, which involves the teacher using strong verbal or gestural hints about expected responses. Teachers often use this move to provide a substantial amount of support for students to participate or when attempting to make material more memorable (Hammond & Gibbons, 2005). Additionally, through appropriation, the teacher may incorporate the language and tools used by their learners in their own dialogue for their own purposes. When doing so, teachers typically recast the wording of the student into more academically appropriate discourse. This reshaping of students' contributions allows the student to be a co-participant in the discourse, but it also enables the teacher to effectively move the discourse forward (de Oliveira & Athanases, 2017). At times, the teacher may incorporate elaboration, which involves supplementing students' contributions with extra information. Elaboration can also be used to ask students to provide more details for their own contributions, which allows them to continue their involvement in the discourse. Additionally, the teacher may use recapping to give a brief summary of the main points of an activity, lesson, or interaction. This can be very helpful for students as it provides them with a connection between key concepts, highlights the information students should have gathered from the activity, lesson, or interaction, and provides students with a clear focus for future learning. There has been increased interest in interactional scaffolding in research in both primary (de Oliveira, Jones, & Smith, 2020) and secondary (Johnson, 2019) classrooms. In fact, de Oliveira, Jones, and Smith (2020) found additional interactional scaffolding moves than the ones found by earlier research and have established a model that teachers can utilize when integrating this type of classroom discourse support (see Figure 2).

2.2.3 Utilizing Students' L1 in the Classroom

Closely related to incorporating students' FOK in the classroom is the idea of utilizing students' L1 in the classroom. Over the years, various scholars have investigated the use of students' first language in multilingual contexts (e.g., Polio & Duff, 1994; Ramos, 2005; Rolin-Ianziti & Varshney, 2008) and advocated for creating classroom spaces that support students' bilingual and biliteracy development (Gallo, 2014; Martínez et al., 2008; Reyes, 2012). One of the first studies to examine the use of L1 in teaching came from Cook (2001), *Using the First Language in the Classroom*. In this important piece, Cook disentangled arguments against the use of L1 and put forth several ways that the L1 could be used in the classroom as a valuable resource (e.g., convey meaning, explain grammar, collaborative learning).

1. **Linking to prior experience and pointing to new experiences** – Connects to students' in and out-of-school experiences and previous learning to current instruction, preparing students for what will follow.

2. **Recapping** – Briefly summarizes the major points of the interaction.

3. **Appropriation** – Utilizes language and tools previously used.

4. **Recasting** – Puts what students say into academically appropriate discourse.

5. **Cued elicitation** – Offers strong hints (e.g., spoken or gestural) about desired responses.

6. **Moving conversation forward** – Provides students with opportunities to say more.

7. **Probing** – Follows-up after a student responds to an initial question, allowing a student to add new information or expand on their answer.

8. **Elaboration** – Supplements contributions with additional information.

9. **Clarification** – Clarifies what students say.

10. **Purposeful repetition** - Draws attention, repeats so all can hear, and provides cues to self-correct or extend thoughts.

Figure 2 Interactional scaffolding moves (based on de Oliveira, Jones, & Smith, 2020)

Following this study, other scholars (e.g., Cummins, 2007; Gort & Pontier, 2013) investigating the use of L1 in the classroom also identified benefits for MLs, including cognitive, emotional, social, and cultural. Research has shown that using the L1 in the classroom can play an important role in developing students' cognitive potential. Central to this finding is the concept of transfer (Cummins, 2005) and the idea that MLs have the ability to transfer their existing metalinguistic and metacognitive skills and strategies from their L1 to their learning of English (Cummins, 2001, 2007) which can contribute to their language development and overall academic success. In order to promote this transfer, researchers call for teachers to explicitly teach language transfer (e.g., systematic attention to cognate relationships across languages; Cunningham & Graham, 2000; de Oliveira, Gilmetdinova, & Pelaez-Morales, 2015).

Apart from supporting students' cognitive growth, utilizing the L1 in the classroom has been identified as a resource for developing students' emotional, social, and cultural capital. By using students' L1, teachers are conveying to children that their proficiency in the L1 "is an important accomplishment that is acknowledged and appreciated within the classroom" (Cummins, 2005, p. 588). Additionally, when teachers build on student's L1 as a source of prior knowledge, they recognize the skills and knowledge that students possess across languages, which can send affirmative messages about the value of knowing and learning multiple languages (Cook, 2007; Cummins, 2001, 2007;) and offset the stigma associated with speaking another language that multilingual students may encounter in and out of school (Bean et al., 2003). Essentially, by bringing students' first languages into the classroom, students are shown that all languages and cultures are respected and are a vital component of a safe and welcoming environment (Bean et al., 2003; de Oliveira, Gilmetdinova, & Pelaez-Morales, 2015; Edstrom, 2006), underscoring the fact that native and nonnative-English speakers bring different yet complementary strengths to the classroom.

More recently, research has focused on the use of translanguaging with multilingual learners (Morales, Schissel, & López-Gopar, 2020; Poza, 2017). Translanguaging includes pedagogical practices that use bilingualism as a resource (García & Kleyn, 2013). More specifically, pedagogical translanguaging refers to "a theoretical and instructional approach that aims at improving language and content competences in school contexts by using resources from the learner's whole linguistic repertoire" (Cenoz & Gorter, 2021, p. 1). The use of pedagogical translanguaging allows multilingual learners to employ all of their linguistic resources to increase their participation in classrooms and improve language and content development. With the goal of developing multilingualism, pedagogical translanguaging highlights an integrated approach to languages and multilingual learners' use of their full linguistic knowledge to further their linguistic and academic learning. There is evidence in the research literature to support using students' L1 in the classroom and pedagogical translanguaging as key parts of the teaching and learning process for MLs, also emphasizing a multilingual approach to language development rather than a monolingual approach that has been the "norm" in the TESOL field for many years now (Ortega, 2013).

2.2.4 Using Multimodal Instruction

Incorporating multimodal instruction in the classroom is an additional practice that enacts culturally sustaining pedagogies. Teachers are being urged to move past paper-based print texts to a more expanded view of instruction (Lenters & Winters, 2013) that can better support their students. This expanded view is one that encompasses multiple modes including image, writing, gesture, gaze, speech, and posture (Jewitt, 2009) for meaning making across content areas. It is important to understand that often one mode alone fails to capture the entire meaning, as meaning resides in the combined effects of the different modes working together in a communicative event (Kress et al., 2001). Multimodal instruction is particularly important for MLs as it has the potential to enhance and expand their understanding of texts (Ajayi, 2009). Rather than relying on a purely linguistic view of literacy, MLs can engage in complex literacy practices by engaging with multiple points of entry into texts (Jewitt, 2005). Rather than starting with the language provided in print, students can opt to analyze visuals, review the typography, or interpret the layout first. This means that instead of simply lecturing on a particular topic, teachers are now charged with incorporating images, gestures, and written texts in their lessons.

Research has shown that multimodal teaching practices afford MLs with the opportunity to successfully comprehend higher level content, navigate complex activities and assignments, and participate fully in the classroom in such a way as to confirm their identities (Garton & Copland, 2019; Lenters & Winters, 2013; Pacheco & Smith, 2015; Takeuchi, 2015; Yi & Choi, 2015). Furthermore, by utilizing multiple modes, teachers can purposefully tap into students' strengths, lived experiences, and sociocultural knowledge (Ajayi, 2009).

For instance, Papas and others (2009) focused on multimodal scientific activities that elementary students were involved in to advance their scientific thinking and aid in their literacy development. Students were engaged in various activities including listening to dialogically enacted read-alouds of information books for children, participating in hands-on explorations, enacting the roles of scientific phenomena by "becoming" scientific entities and "behaving" as part of a system, writing/drawing in a journal, creating an ongoing class semantic map, and finally, writing and illustrating an information book on a topic of choice at the end of a unit (Papas et al., 2009). By examining the student-created books, they concluded that the children made substantial gains in their scientific thinking. The books displayed the rich content that children acquired through the multimodal activities that were conducted throughout the unit.

2.2.5 Applying a Functional Approach to Language Development

Applying a functional approach to language development is another practice that enacts culturally sustaining pedagogies as it seeks to purposefully maintain the practices of students while also expanding their knowledge and abilities. This particular practice encourages students to explore meaning in texts as they engage in classroom discussions about language. Guided by the teacher, students learn to use a metalanguage for identifying and describing the linguistic choices made by the authors and the language patterns that are present throughout the text. This approach can be incorporated across contexts and is particularly helpful for multilingual students as they are able to focus on how language works while developing their linguistic repertoires in more than one language.

A functional approach to language development (de Oliveira, 2016; de Oliveira & Westerlund, 2021; Fang & Schleppegrell, 2008) draws on systemic functional linguistics (SFL), a meaning-based theory of language, in order to provide teachers with ways to talk about and address the language demands of the content areas for multilingual learners. Part of addressing the language demands is supporting students' development of academic language, or the language used for schooling purposes, which exists on the same continuum as everyday language, or the language used for social purposes in everyday life (Schleppegrell, 2013). In this process of supporting the development of academic language, educators must be knowledgeable about the language in and through which they teach as they are tasked with scaffolding multilingual students' learning of both the content and the language. Along these lines, research has consistently shown how important it is to bridge everyday language with academic language for understanding content (e.g., de Oliveira, 2016; Gibbons, 2006; Khote, 2018).

This approach has been shown to be particularly useful for MLs' development of academic language across the grades (see, for example, Brisk, 2015; Brisk & Zisselsberger, 2011; Gebhard, 2019; Moore & Schleppegrell, 2014). For example, Symons and Bian (2022) found that teachers can use their metalinguistic awareness and knowledge of SFL to scaffold comprehension for MLs and amplify their metalinguistic awareness in discussions of texts. Moore and Schleppegrell (2014) found that a functional metalanguage helps teachers and students look closely at language to see patterns that are connected to categories of meaning and, therefore, explore with MLs the language features of the texts they read and write, supporting their overall understanding and language development.

The notion of genre is instrumental within this approach as it focuses explicitly on academic language development in the content of literacy activities, allowing the discussion of the social purposes of texts and the ways in which language is presented and organized differently to achieve specific goals. Genre has been defined as a "staged, goal-oriented social process" (Martin, 2009, p. 13). It is "staged" because it requires more than one phase of meaning to work through a genre; it is "goal-oriented" because the various phases are designed in order to accomplish something; and it is "social" because genres are undertaken with others interactively (Martin, 2009). The notion of genre was utilized to design what is now known as genre pedagogy or a genre-based approach, with a focus on enhancing literacy teaching and learning across disciplines and grade levels.

Genre pedagogy is often used to scaffold literacy instruction by means of the Teaching and–Learning Cycle (TLC; Hyland, 2007; Martin, 2009; Rose & Martin, 2012). The TLC (see Figure 3), a pedagogical framework which helps

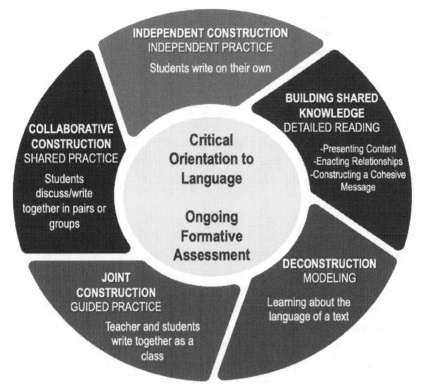

Figure 3 Enactment of a functional approach to language development:
The teaching and learning cycle

learners develop explicit knowledge about language, is centered on the principle of "guidance through interaction in the context of shared experiences" (Martin & Rose, 2005, p. 253). This principle refers to the guidance provided by teachers in talking, reading, and writing about a particular text in the context of a shared experience – a common reading, field trip or activity, movie, science experiment, school event, and so on. Students write about a common experience, not about something that they experienced on their own, which allows the teacher (and peers) to provide support. This is why the concept of a shared experience is so critical for students, especially MLs. Following the phases of the TLC, teachers and students first build shared knowledge through Detailed Reading, then move on to the deconstruction of mentor texts followed by a process known as joint construction, and finish up with collaborative and independent construction.

The TLC takes students through various phases: building shared knowledge through Detailed Reading, deconstruction of mentor texts, joint construction, collaborative construction, and independent construction. Though the TLC allows students different points of entry and enables teachers to start at any one of these phases, it is important to build shared knowledge about a new genre by starting with the building of shared knowledge and deconstruction. Following these phases is important so that all students are prepared to write in the expected genres. Just giving students a topic or prompt and asking them to write is not teaching writing but assessing what students already are able to do with writing. This process can be recursive and repeated as students become more familiar with specific genres. **Building Shared Knowledge through Detailed Reading** (de Oliveira, Klassen, & Maune, 2015; Derewianka & Jones, 2016) develops students' knowledge of the content and context of particular texts. Students also build a critical orientation to language by learning about language and about the genre while teachers assess student learning at all phases of activity. Detailed Reading involves purposefully selecting short passages from the focal text and guiding students to read them sentence-by-sentence. Many classrooms rely on complex informational reading selections, which is why this phase of the TLC is so critical in helping students understand the texts they read. Students and teachers explore how the text is written and how it accomplishes its goals through language choices. Detailed Reading focuses on classroom inter-actions with students, conducting read-alouds, identifying language features, focus-ing on grammatical expressions, target vocabulary, and main ideas. They focus on three areas of meaning: *presenting content, enacting relationships*, and *construct-ing a cohesive message*, and teacher and students explore the text as it is written, without any simplification (de Oliveira & Schleppegrell, 2015). Table 1 presents these three areas of meaning, questions to guide language discussion, and the focus of language related to each area of meaning, described in more detail next.

When we look at how a text *presents content*, we explore the Participants (typically expressed through nouns) engaged in Processes (typically expressed through verbs) under certain Circumstances (typically expressed through prepos-itional and adverbial phrases) (de Oliveira & Schleppegrell, 2015; Halliday & Matthiessen, 2014). Participants are the entities involved in the process, typically realized in noun groups (e.g., *the magnet, many metal objects, a scientific phenom-enon*). These participants take on different semantic roles in different process types. Processes can be categorized into five main types, expressed through verbs:

- **doing verbs** represent actions such as *participate* and *run*
- **relating verbs** show relationships between ideas such as *is* and *has*
- **thinking verbs** represent thought such as *think, know, consider*
- **feeling verbs** represent feelings such as *admire, love, like*
- **saying verbs** indicate what someone or something has said such as *say, tell, ask*.

Table 1 Detailed Reading: Areas of meaning, questions, and focus of analysis

Area of Meaning	Question to Guide Language Discussion	Focus of Language
Presenting content	✓ What is happening? ✓ Who are the people or things involved? ✓ What are the circumstances surrounding events?	Sentence Constituents: Participants, processes, circumstances
Enacting relationships	✓ What are the roles and relationships taken up by participants?	Mood choices: · Declarative · Interrogative · Imperative Modality
Constructing a cohesive message	✓ How is the text organized? ✓ How is the language used?	Theme/New Cohesion

Note. Table is based on de Oliveira and Schleppegrell (2015).

Processes also take place around circumstances (of time, space, conditions, purpose, etc.), typically realized in adverbs (e.g., *finally, separately*) or prepositional phrases (e.g., *around the corner, with a fork*). Teachers and students explore participants, processes, and circumstances in clauses to reveal how content is presented.

Texts also e*nact relationships* through mood and modality choices. Teachers and students explore the presence or absence of the subject and finite elements of the clauses and in what order they occur with respect to one another (Halliday & Matthiessen, 2014). These are important because they realize the grammatical choice of the *mood* of a clause: either declarative, interrogative, or imperative. Examining the mood system allows us to identify how and why an author or speaker chose to make statements (typically expressed in declarative mood), ask questions (typically expressed in interrogative mood), or declare commands (typically expressed in imperative mood). Another area to examine is *modality*, which concerns the different ways in which someone expresses evaluation, attitudes, and judgments of various kinds. Modality allows us to express possibility, certainty, normality, usuality, necessity, and obligation. This includes modal verbs (e.g., *should, might, could*), modal adjectives (e.g., *frequent, usual*), modal adverbs (e.g., *probably, certainly, typically*), and modal nouns (e.g., *condition, necessity*). Evaluative vocabulary enables the construction of stance and judgment. Mood, modality, and evaluative vocabulary express meanings that enact a relationship between reader and listener and writer and speaker.

When we look at how a text *constructs a cohesive message*, we can examine Given/New patterns. "Given" is the first experiential element of the clause and "New" encompasses the remaining bit of the clause (Halliday & Matthiessen, 2014). One very useful strategy is tracking the given patterns (also called thematic development) through texts, which, in part, helps organize the overall text as it moves from paragraph to paragraph and within the paragraph. Another important area to explore is cohesion, the way a text hangs together with the support of cohesive devices such as pronouns (e.g., *they, that, her*), synonyms and substitutes (e.g., *exemplar-ideal; The Declaration of Independence – this document*), and connectors (e.g., *and, despite, if*).

Deconstruction is the next phase of the TLC. During Deconstruction, teachers introduce mentor texts from a focal genre which students are expected to read and write. The teacher uses demonstration, modeling, and discussions about text purpose, organization, and language features in order to scaffold students' understanding about language and meaning (Derewianka & Jones, 2016). Teachers approach Deconstruction from various angles, sometimes incorporating graphic organizers (e.g., Brisk, Hodgson-Drysdale, & O'Connor, 2011), facilitating whole-class discussions (e.g., Palincsar & Schleppegrell, 2014), highlighting and underlining specific linguistic features (e.g., de Oliveira & Lan 2014; Schulze 2011), or drawing on manipulatives (Brisk & Zisselsberger 2011) to foster an understanding of language and content. Most recently, after their work in K-5 classrooms, both Brisk (2014) and de Oliveira (2017) included an additional, optional phase entitled *collaborative construction*. Collaborative construction can be a significant phase in the TLC for the early grades, as described by de Oliveira, Jones, and Smith (2020).

The next phase is **Joint Construction**, in which the teacher and students work together to write a text from the focal genre, using the text they deconstructed as a model. During this guided practice, teacher and students are writing together as a class and the teacher provides a bridge for students between the everyday language they are accustomed to using for social purposes and the academic language appropriate for the text in the new genre (de Oliveira, 2017). When providing a bridge for students, the teacher draws their attention to the purpose, stages, and language features of the genre, with the idea of gradually handing over responsibility to students in the third and final phases of the TLC. Joint Construction typically takes place as a whole-class collaborative writing activity (e.g., Caplan & Farling, 2017; Gebhard, Harman, & Seger 2007), but it can also work well in small-group and one-on-one settings (e.g., Harman 2013; Kerfoot & Van Heerden, 2015). Regardless of the setting, this phase provides the teacher with a critical opportunity to demonstrate how different genre features come together to form a cohesive text. Joint Construction is a critical phase in the TLC which can make a significant difference in the preparation of MLs for writing independently (Caplan & Farling, 2017).

In the final two phases, students apply what they learned in the initial teacher-directed phases. **Collaborative Construction** provides students with an opportunity to work with their peers in pairs or small groups to create a text together, as they brainstorm and negotiate ideas, write, and revise (e.g., Chung & Walsh 2006; Woo, Chu, & Li, 2013). The teacher provides support to the pairs or groups as needed throughout the phase. This phase is especially important for younger learners who are in the process of developing reading and writing skills but can be used with students at any age. During **Independent Construction**, students are charged with writing a text in the new genre on their own, drawing on both the text they deconstructed and the texts they jointly created with the teacher and peer(s) in previous phases of the cycle.

A functional approach to language development has received increased attention over the past fifteen years in the United States. A renewed attention to this approach occurred with the publication of the new WIDA English Language Development Standards Framework (WIDA, 2020). In December 2020, WIDA, an organization dedicated to the academic achievement of MLs, published a new edition of the WIDA English Language Development Standards Framework. The revised edition offers a renewed commitment to equity for MLs and includes a functional approach to language as one of its "Big Ideas," key premises that informed the development of the standards framework and should guide classroom instruction for MLs, along with building on students' linguistic and cultural assets and bridging content and language in collaborative environments. While this approach may not be new in other parts of the world, it is new to many teachers in the US context in which most of our experiences have been.

3 Practices in Action: Evidence and Examples from Pedagogy-Informed Research Studies

Our own asset-based, pedagogy-informed research studies counter pervasive deficit approaches towards the teaching and learning of MLs, focusing on practices and ways of being, and how they can and are included meaningfully in classrooms. In the past twenty years, this asset-based pedagogical research has been increasingly important in elementary and secondary schools in order to make a more explicit commitment to sustaining the valued practices and ways of being of multilingual learners (e.g., de Oliveira, Jones, & Smith, 2020; de Oliveira, Jones, & Smith, 2021). We draw on these research studies to show various examples of culturally sustaining teaching practices (CSTP).

There are five main CSTPs that we include here, presented in Figure 4.

1. Drawing on students' funds of knowledge in the classroom builds background and fosters connections.
2. Incorporating interactional scaffolding moves creates spaces for meaningful classroom interactions.
3. Using MLs' home languages and cultures as a resource supports language development.
4. Multimodal instruction creates message abundance that provides challenging content, not simplified instruction.
5. A functional approach to language development expands MLs' meaning-making resources.

3.1 Culturally Sustaining Teaching Practices for Young Multilingual Learners

3.1.1 Drawing on Students' Funds of Knowledge in the Classroom Builds Background and Fosters Connections

This practice includes teachers' connections to students' lives, backgrounds, and experiences in instruction. MLs' home experiences are strengths that can

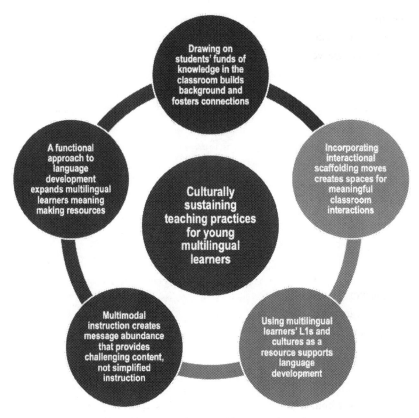

Figure 4 Culturally sustaining teaching practices for young MLs

be drawn upon, and first-hand experiences with families allow MLs to show what they know. The example comes from a study in a fifth-grade classroom. We collaborated with the teacher, Ms. Jana Cabana, for three years when we worked in Florida. She first taught first grade and the year after the initial case study moved to teaching fifth grade. In fifth grade, Ms. Cabana had two classes. At the time of the studies, she had more than fifteen years of teaching experience. Together, the classes were comprised of forty-four students, forty of whom spoke a language other than English at home. As part of the Spanish pathway in the international studies magnet program, many students were bilingual English/Spanish speakers. However, there were a number of other languages present as well, including French, German, Arabic, Russian, and Mandarin, among others. This classroom excerpt shows Ms. Cabana drawing on students' FOK about their family's histories and ancestors. The context was a lesson on traditions.

Excerpt 1

1. Teacher: because for number four, we did the country origin, but we talked we said we've learned about culture, right? When we said the cultural region that, we know that there's a lot more to culture than just where you come from. So I wanna stick with number four for a minute. Thank you. So for number four, what is something else about someone's culture that we can talk about?
2. Student: Tradition?
3. Teacher: Okay. Traditions. Let's go for traditions. So how about favorite tradition? Favorite family tradition.
4. Students: Christmas, Christmas.
5. Teacher: Christmas okay. So let's go ahead and, put for Christmas.
6. Students: Merry christmas merry christmas . . . family family.
7. Teacher: So that would stay as a four,
8. Students: Traditions . . . shhhh . . . It's an H.
9. Teacher: C yeah C H C H R okay alright perfect. Jack thank you. Lisa you're up next. Now we're not done with culture just yet. What else makes up culture?
10. Students: . . . Colombia . . . Food?
11. Teacher: Mauricio?
12. Mauricio: Their descent like ummm.
13. Teacher: Shhh. Wait hold. Mauricio is speaking.
14. Marteas: Their descent like umm if you're Peruvian than there's a chance that you're also ecodescent.
15. Teacher: Okay.
16. Marteas: like if you're Mexican there's a chance that you're also miodescent.
17. Teacher: Very good. So when they talk about descent going far down your family, where are you? You guys know that? Have you ever done your family history? Or have your parents shared that with you?
18. Juli: I know that I know like my mom's like grandpa.
19. Students: I know my grandfather is 30 percent Irish. It's like all of that in Colombia.
20. Teacher: Okay. So you have a long, strong line in Colombia, okay? And Matias, do you happen to know?
21. Matias: My great grandpa is from Germany.
22. Students: Germany?
23. Teacher: Okay. So let's go ahead then and put that. I'll wait. So we're gonna go ahead and put four, right? Because we're still talking about culture and country of origin.

This example shows how Ms. Cabana is using students' FOK to get to know students' backgrounds and experiences and help draw on these skills in classrooms. Bringing students' FOK to the forefront of a lesson is a strategy to build student engagement through connecting personal interests with curriculum content. Ms. Cabana recalls that students' cultures are not just their country of origin and encourages them to think beyond geographical borders. She prompts students to offer ideas and the discussion turns to traditions and sharing family histories. When she asks "have you ever done your family history?", Ms. Cabana sees the importance of valuing students' home experiences. Family histories are relevant to learning more deeply about traditions. Acknowledging and incorporating personal histories develops a bridge for students to see themselves as individuals, parts of different communities, and necessary participants in the learning process.

This practice enriches students' understanding of academic content while also motivating them during classroom activities and offers teachers opportunities to see a more complex view of families, bridging home and school. The use of this culturally sustaining teaching practice with MLs in particular can contribute to improving the classroom climate as the teacher gets to know the student in a broader context through more active and personal interactions ('t Gilde & Volman, 2021). It also better supports academic learning as students engage in discussions about their experiences and backgrounds that bridge into the formal curriculum.

3.1.2 Incorporating Interactional Scaffolding Moves Creates Spaces for Meaningful Classroom Interactions

Incorporating interactional scaffolding moves has shown to be a critical practice in the education of young MLs (see de Oliveira, Jones, & Smith, 2020; Hammond & Gibbons, 2005). Interactional scaffolding is instrumental in how teachers engage students in the classroom and creates meaningful interactions. Young MLs need to productively engage in classroom discourse and express their knowledge and understanding of content. Teachers can create a positive classroom culture in which students feel that their participation and contributions are valued.

This exchange comes from a first-grade classroom that Ms. Cabana taught. At the time of this study, Ms. Cabana had twenty-three students in her classroom, four of whom were receiving English for speakers of other languages (ESOL) services. Two of these four students had a home language of Portuguese, while the other two identified Spanish as their home language. Twelve others identified as bilingual, although they did not receive ESOL services. In the United

States, the great majority (3.6 million) of MLs speak Spanish at home (NCES, 2020), and this was reflected in Ms. Cabana's first-grade classroom, where most of the bilingual students spoke Spanish and English, with parents from countries such as Cuba, Mexico, Argentina, Spain, and Honduras.

Excerpt 2

1. Ms. Cabana: Since last week I have been thinking about this one line that we read in Johnny Appleseed. It's on page nineteen. If you look at the illustration you see where Johnny Appleseed is holding the seeds. I see something glowing around them. Who has ever had an apple before?
2. Students: [All the students raise their hands.]
3. Ms. C: Have you ever seen the seeds?
4. Ss: [Multiple students call out mixed answers over each other, including, "Yes!" and "I ate them!"]
5. Ms. C: I want you to think about the time that you held or you looked at your apple seeds. Now look at Johnny. When he holds his seeds, what do you see glowing around his seeds?
6. Student 1: Gold.
7. Ms. C: Has anyone ever seen apple seeds with gold around them?
8. Ss: [Multiple students call out mixed answers over each other.]
9. Ms. C: Go back to page nineteen and reread it to yourself and tell me what the author says about the seeds. ["He grinned as if the seeds were gold." (Harrison, 2001: 19)]. What does the author say about the seeds? Turn to a neighbor and tell them what the author says about the seeds.
10. Ss: [Students talk to each other while Ms. Cabana circulates, listens to conversations, and provides feedback.]
11. Ms. C: I want to hear what you are thinking and sharing with your partner. Who would like to share? What was the author trying to say? Does the author mean the seeds were really gold or does he mean something else?
12. Student 2: He means something else.
13. Ms. C: Okay. Can you tell me why you think that? Or, what do you think the author means?
14. Student 2: He means that it's gold for him.
15. Ms. C: Okay. Any other ideas?
16. Student 3: It looks like gold, but it's not really gold.
17. Ms. C: Okay, so what does that mean? Gold is what to people? "As if they were gold . . ." We used a really important word last week and it starts with a V. We talked about how gold is a way to show that there is a lot of what? A long time ago when people had gold, they were very . . .
18. Ss: Rich.

19. Ms. C: Gold was very . . .
20. Ss: Valuable!
21. Ms. C: We talked about how gold might not be valuable to everyone. Valuable is something that is important to you and something that is very special.

This exchange shows Ms. Cabana incorporating several interactional scaffolding moves to create spaces for meaningful classroom interactions. This exchange shows her asking students to interpret the figurative language and infer meaning from both the written text and the corresponding images (e.g., turn 5). The use of varied participant structures allowed students opportunities to contribute their ideas to the conversation (turn 9). Ms. Cabana used the interactional scaffolding moves of moving the conversation forward (turn 15), probing (turn 13), and cued elicitation (turns 17 and 19). Probing is used as a follow-up question after a student responds to an initial question, allowing the student to add new information or expand on their answer. With Student 2, a young ML (identified as a Level 4 ELL), she specifically asked an additional question to help her say more, using the probing move (turn 13). This move is especially important for young multilingual learners so they have opportunities for continuous participation in classroom discussions. Cued elicitation is when the teacher offers strong hints (e.g., spoken or gestural) about desired responses, as in "Gold was very . . .." After deconstructing this text, Ms. Cabana encouraged students to make personal connections, asking them to think of someone that is personally like gold to them. Students eagerly named individuals specific to their lives, such as best friends, family members, and family pets. Linking this to students' prior experiences, Ms. Cabana moved the conversation forward to focus on a shared connection with which everyone could relate (de Oliveira, Jones, & Smith, 2020).

3.1.3 Using Multilingual Learners' Home Languages and Cultures As a Resource Supports Language Development

Using MLs' home languages and cultures as a resource is a key component of teaching this population of students, as many years of research have shown (García & Li, 2014). This practice fosters the use of students' L1s in the classroom, including in teachers' discourse, students' contributions, and lesson planning and delivery to emphasize an integrated approach to language and content learning.

The following excerpts are taken from a kindergarten classroom. This case study was conducted in a kindergarten classroom in a school of 30 percent identified as ELLs, mostly from Latino/a backgrounds in Indiana (see de Oliveira, Gilmetdinova, & Pelaez-Morales, 2015; de Oliveira, Klassen, & Gilmetdinova, 2015). The classroom was composed of twenty-three students, eight of whom were classified as ELLs from Latino/a backgrounds. The eight ELLs had different levels of English proficiency with three being fully bilingual and at least three being recent arrivals to the US and speaking little to no English. Ruby Li was the kindergarten teacher, who at the time of the study had recently completed a licensure program in English Language Learning (ELL), so she had developed specific skills and strategies for working with students whose home languages are not English. Her use of Spanish in the classroom is more fully described in de Oliveira, Gilmetdinova, and Pelaez-Morales (2015).

Excerpt 3

1. Ms. Li: Remember how we talked about our relatives yesterday? Not immediate ... that immediate family, the really close ones ... that this boy probably didn't even know, right? But they can still talk about grandpa's memories. We can look at old pictures and try to imagine people in them. Let's look at those pictures of your family, a long time ago. Well, it might make us cry, but that's ok. Do you ever have your mom look at old pictures of grandma or grandpa and get sad because they miss them? So they are looking at old pictures. [and a little later]

2. Ms. Li: Who has at least one grandma? ¿Quién tiene una abuela? [Who has a grandma?] Everybody has a grandma? Todos tienen una abuela? [Everyone has a grandma?] ¿Sí? [Yes?] Yes? Or who has a grandpa? Raise your hand if you have a grandpa. ¿Quién tiene un abuelo? [Who has a grandpa?] If you don't have a grandpa, then do this for your grandma. Ok? Si no tienes un abuelo, puedes dibujar tu abuela. [If you don't have a grandpa, you can draw your grandma.] If you have both, you can choose one.

Excerpt 4

1. Ms. Li: In this top picture, everybody point to the top picture. It says what? Jocelyn, read out loud.

2. J: This is me.

3. Ms. Li: This is me. Good. Draw you in that box. Dibuja tu cuerpo.

4. [after some time]

5. Ms. Li: This is called "family and social health" ... Families that work and play. How do these families work and play? Raise your hand and tell me how do these families work and play. Malia?

6. Malia: They recycle.

7 Ms. Li: They recycle. Very nice. Kory?

8 Kory: They clean.

9 Ms. Li: What else, Alex?

10 Alex: Store

11 Ms. Li: They go to the store together. They fly kites together. Jaime, ¿tu sabes? ¿Que hacen juntos?

12 Jaime: Eat.

13 Ms. Li: Muy bien, they eat together! Guadalupe?

14 Guadalupe: Go shopping together.

15 Ms. Li: They go shopping together; good job!

The two excerpts show Ms. Li's use of students' home language and culture as a pedagogical practice to apply the linguistic repertoires of her MLs in order to teach both rigorous content and language for academic use. These examples show the use of connections to children's own experiences to improve literacy learning. In Excerpt 3, we can observe Ms. Li providing students with instructions in English (If you don't have a grandpa, then do this for your grandma. Ok?), followed by the same instructions in Spanish (Si no tienes un abuelo, puedes dibujar tu abuela. [If you don't have a grandpa, you can draw your grandma]). In this same excerpt, we see that she also is asking questions to elicit information from the students, therefore also clarifying content that MLs were exposed to during the lesson:

> Who has at least one grandma? ¿Quién tiene una abuela? [Who has a grandma?] Everybody has a grandma? Todos tienen una abuela? [Everyone has a grandma?] ¿Sí? [Yes?] Yes? Or who has a grandpa? Raise your hand if you have a grandpa. ¿Quién tiene un abuelo? [Who has a grandpa?].

In excerpt 4, Ms. Li also combines English and Spanish instructions in turn 3 (Draw you in that box. Dibuja tu cuerpo.) By using both languages in the instructions, Ms. Li is legitimatizing the role of the students' home language in the classroom. Her goal in using Spanish in many instances appears to be to clarify instructions.

While the Spanish Ms. Li uses is not complex or always accurate, she manages to communicate her messages clearly. Most importantly, she developed her knowledge of Spanish to be able to support her young MLs. Most of her language use involves vocabulary items and helping students understand instructions. She also actively relied on peer support from English and Spanish-proficient students to clarify something to a less proficiency student, to translate a concept, or even to learn new vocabulary herself. Ms. Li says she has learned to use Spanish for her classroom instruction over the years because she has seen the benefit of this practice for her Spanish-speaking bilingual learners.

3.1.4 Multimodal Instruction Creates Message Abundance That Provides Challenging Content, Not Simplified Instruction

Multimodal instruction affords MLs the opportunity to more fully participate in the classroom (Pacheco & Smith, 2015). Multimodal activities are especially important for young MLs as they are tasked with learning both content and language simultaneously. Teachers can no longer reduce learning to paper-based resources (Lotherington & Jenson, 2011) so, by utilizing multiple modes, students can use their strengths, experiences, and knowledge.

We use examples of our work with a second-grade pre-service teacher, Crista, who was completing her student teaching experience at an elementary school in Florida. At the time of this lesson, she was a senior pursuing a degree in elementary education with a specialization in exceptional student education (ESE) with additional endorsements in reading and ESOL. The class was part of a magnet program, which means the students receive instruction in English for two-thirds of the day and in Spanish for one-third of the day. The science instruction was taught in English. There was a total of 28 students, four of whom were labeled as ESOL learners and half the class identified as bilingual.

Crista worked in collaboration with her supervisors from the university to plan the unit of instruction on living things. The lesson is one of a series of lessons that were implemented over the course of several days. This lesson was framed by three main objectives: After the lesson, students will be able to (1) identify the main parts of the plant, (2) acknowledge why the leaves are the most important parts of the plant, and (3) describe the process of photosynthesis. This lesson used multiple modes to present information and focused on student's engagement in various multimodal and multisensory activities to help develop their content knowledge (see Table 2).

To start this lesson, Crista engaged students in a discussion in which they reviewed information about the basic needs of living things and the parts of the plant that they had learned the previous day. Crista asked students, "What do plants need to survive?" to initiate the discussion, and several students volunteered their answers. She wrote the students' answers on the board so that she could maintain a list of notes that students could then copy down in their notebooks to reference when needed throughout the lesson and the remainder of the unit. After the discussion to review previous knowledge, Crista worked

Table 2 "Parts of a plant – importance of the leaves" lesson

Timeline	Teacher	Students	Multimodal and *Multisensory* Elements
12:00	Facilitates a review discussion – basic needs of living things and the parts of a plant.	Volunteer information about the needs of living things and the parts of a plant according to what they learned previously.	Speech and writing *Auditory and reading/writing*
12:10	Guides students in drawing/labeling the parts of a flower on the whiteboard.	Draw/label the parts of a flower in their notebook while also helping to identify the parts in discussion.	Speech, writing, image, and gesture *Auditory, reading/writing, visual, and kinesthetic*
12:15	Shows pictures of real plants/plant parts on the smart board. Engages students in conversation about how the parts of a plant relate to body parts.	View the images and make comments/answer questions.	Image and speech *Visual and auditory*
12:25	Writes the word *photosynthesis* on the board, breaks it down to show that *photo* means light and *synthesis* means to put together.	Copy down the new vocabulary term in their notebooks, highlighting the two parts of the word.	Writing and speech *Reading/writing and auditory*

12:30	Leads students on a walking field trip. Points out the different parts of a variety of plants, shows epiphytes, and asks questions.	Participate in walking field trip by examining the plants and plant parts. Answer questions about different plants that they see.	Gesture, gaze, and speech *Kinesthetic, visual, and auditory*
12:40	Directs students to pick out a leaf to bring back to the science lab for another activity.	Select a leaf to bring back to the classroom for further investigation.	Speech and gaze *Auditory, visual, and kinesthetic*
12:45	Gives instructions to students to complete a leaf rub in their notebooks using the leaf they selected.	Place the leaf under one sheet of paper and shade over it with a green crayon. Pay special attention to the detailed veins of the leaf.	Speech, writing, and gaze *Auditory, reading/writing, visual, and kinesthetic*
12:50	Instructs students to complete a worksheet titled, "Observe a Leaf."	Complete the assigned worksheet.	Speech and writing *Auditory and reading/writing*
12:50	Calls students to the back of the classroom (in groups) to examine leaves that she had placed under microscopes.	Take turns viewing the leaves under the microscope to notice the veins, the size, color, etc.	Speech and gaze *Auditory, visual, and kinesthetic*
1:00	Presents students with a summarizing activity where they must complete the sentence, "In this investigation, I learned _____."	Write the sentence starter and their response in their notebooks. Volunteer to verbally share their responses with the class.	Speech and writing *Auditory and reading/writing*

with students to draw and label the parts of the flower on the white board. As Crista did this on the white board, students copied it down in their notebooks. During this process, as students identified the different parts of the flower, Crista showed pictures of real plants/plant parts on the smart board. Crista engaged students in conversation about how the parts of the plant relate to parts of the body. For example, she helped students make the connection between the stem of a plant and the spine of a body, the veins of the body and the veins in a leaf. Finally, Crista wrote the word *photosynthesis* on the board and helped students break it down to show that *photo* means light and *synthesis* means to put together. She used this term to describe how plants use light to put together chemical compounds and turn them into food: "Photosynthesis is how plants eat. They use this process to make their own food. Since they don't have to move around to find food, plants stay in one place, which means they can make their food anywhere" (Field Notes, 3/14).

After this initial work, Crista took the students on a walking field trip through the main gazebo area of their school. During the walking field trip, Crista pointed out the different parts of a variety of plants (e.g., root, stems, leaves). In addition, she showed students epiphytes (a plant that grows off of another plant), as there were many examples of this in the area that they were exploring (see Figure 1). At the end of the field trip, Crista directed students to pick out a leaf to bring back to the science lab for another activity.

Once the students returned to the classroom they were directed to complete a leaf rub in their notebooks using the leaf they selected at the end of the walking field trip (see Figure 5). Students placed the leaf under one sheet of paper in their notebooks and shaded over it with a green crayon. This allowed students to see the details of the leaf including its shape and veins. At this time, Crista emphasized how the veins were the most important part of the leaf because they carry food to the rest of the plant to help it survive.

Following the leaf rub, students participated in three more activities. They were given a worksheet to complete titled "Observe a Leaf." Guided by this worksheet, students described where they found their leaf, the size (measured using a ruler), the texture, the smell, and the color. At the end of the worksheet students completed the sentence starter, "My leaf is important to its plant because ...." While students were completing this worksheet independently at their tables, Crista called groups of students to the back of the classroom to look at leaves that she had placed under microscopes. This activity allowed students to view the veins and cells of the leaves. At the very end of the lesson, the students were directed to go back to their journals to complete a quick summarizing activity. In their notebooks, students completed the following sentence: "In this investigation, I learned _____."

Figure 5 Epiphytes from the walking field trip and a leaf rub

The multimodal and multisensory activities used supported MLs as they worked to develop their language as well as scientific content knowledge. Crista used multiple modes in her teaching to encourage the participation and focus of all learners, especially MLs, while scaffolding their content learning. For instance, Crista was able to engage students by drawing and labeling the flower on the white board (with input from students), while simultaneously displaying images of various plants/plant parts (with labels) on the smart board. This multimodal use of the board allowed students to see the connection between the parts of the plant they had been discussing and the plants that they see outside in their everyday lives. In addition to drawing on the modes of image, speech, and writing, Crista used gestures a great deal to capture students' attention and emphasize important ideas throughout the lesson. For example, when participating in the walking field trip, she constantly pointed to the parts of plants, prompting students to identify what the part was called (Lesson Plan: "Point out the roots, stem, and leaves of different plants. Point out the epiphytes"). This use of gestures required students to draw on the material they had learned and reviewed in class over the past couple of days. Her multimodal instruction provided message abundancy

(Gibbons, 2015) – key ideas being presented in many different ways – to provide challenging content, not simplify instruction.

3.1.5 A Functional Approach to Language Development Expands Multilingual Learners' Meaning-Making Resources

A functional approach to language development offers ways of engaging MLs in exploring meaning in texts through purposeful classroom discussions about language (de Oliveira & Westerlund, 2021). This approach provides a metalanguage for talking about the meanings in authors' language choices. It enables teachers to identify language patterns in order to help young MLs see how language works and expand their meaning making resources.

The excerpts shown next are from a case study conducted with a fourth-grade teacher in Indiana, Karla Dixon. At the time of the study, she had been teaching fourth grade for six years at Campus University School District. Mrs. Dixon taught in a school district with 30 percent culturally and linguistically diverse (CLD) students, including MLs, and 70 percent White backgrounds. Many of the CLD students came from families whose parents were associated with the nearby university, including children of international students and immigrants. Over the course of five years, Mrs. Dixon implemented a functional approach to language development in her classroom in various "phases." Phase 1 focused on reading science texts and developing lessons to address the challenges of science, then moved on to Phase 2 addressing writing instruction about science experiments. Phase 3 focused on talking science, or the classroom discourse about science that supported and challenged MLs (see de Oliveira & Lan, 2014, for more details about each phase). At the time of the study, she had just completed her Master's degree in Literacy and Language Education at a local university.

We use excerpts from her classroom teaching to exemplify how a functional approach can be implemented in the classroom, in this case in the teaching of science. The following are excerpts from class discussions about a science text. At this point in the lesson, Mrs. Dixon and students are going through a text about how animals are classified. Students had been working on the concepts of *participants*, *process*, and *scientific description*, based on systemic functional linguistics, introduced in previous lessons. Mrs. Dixon had explained to students that *participants* are the who or what that is participating in the process, represented as a person(s) or thing(s). A *process* is a verb group that shows what is going on (the *doing*, *thinking*, *saying*, or *being*). The *scientific pattern* is what came after the *doing* or *being processes* that described or explained something about the participants and processes. Students were working on a "language dissection" activity, as Mrs. Dixon named these lessons.

Excerpt 5

1 Mrs. Dixon: *Amphibians are covered with smooth skin.* What so far are we talking about with both of those sentences? Look at Alena's hand; she is writing up!

2 Alena: Like what they have on their body.

3 Mrs. Dixon: What they have on their bodies. Let's see if this continues. Carla, will you bring yours up, #1 go ahead and read it for me.

4 S: *Reptiles are covered with scales.*

5 Mrs. Dixon: *Reptiles are covered with scales.* Again, are we talking about what's on the outside of the body? Edna, bring yours up and read it out loud for us.

6 Ss: *Birds are covered with feathers.*

7 Mrs. Dixon: *Birds are covered with feathers.* Does anybody notice a verb that keeps being repeated for the process? What keeps being repeated, Nora?

8 S: *Covered.*

9 Mrs. Dixon: Yes, we have the word **covered** every time. Is the word **covered** in your process, too, Alena?

10 Alena: Oh, no!

11 Mrs. Dixon: We have a difference here! Is it still the same, are we still talking about the same process?

12 S: Yeah, what it's covered in.

13 Mrs. Dixon: We're still talking about the same thing except that it didn't say covered with fur. What do you think that means, why do you think they didn't use the word covered for this one? They used the word covered for every other one. Do you have an idea, Laura? Why didn't they use the word covered this time? Alena, you are up here; why don't you tell us.

14 Alena: Because they aren't all covered, they could have hair or fur.

15 Mrs. Dixon: Yeah, think about it, they aren't all covered. Are you covered, do we have some hair?

16 S: Yeah.

17 Mrs. Dixon: But we probably wouldn't say covered with hair. We don't look like bears! So they chose not to put covered for this very last one; kind of interesting. Let's see if our second sentence has a pattern, Laura. You guys have fish, so go ahead and read the fish sentence for me. You guys have been great listeners, by the way!

18 S: *They live only in water.*

19 Mrs. Dixon: *They live only in water.* What are we talking about this time? What is the topic of our sentence? What are we talking about, Carla?

20 Kayla: Where they live.

21 Mrs. Dixon: Where they live. Let's see if the second group also talks about where they live. Brian. What you have?

22 S: *They can live on land and in water.*

23 Mrs. Dixon: *They can live on land and in water.* Do you think the authors purposely put these in the same order every time?

24 Ss: Yeah.

25 Mrs. Dixon: Do you think you would have noticed right away that they put them in the same order?

26 Ss: No.

27 Mrs. Dixon: I wouldn't have noticed honestly; but you know what, you may have noticed right away. But sometimes in science books and writing, you're going to see these types of patterns if you look at them carefully. Let's look at the next group to see if it also tells about where they live. Kayla, go ahead.

This exchange exemplifies how the implementation of a functional approach to language development can expand MLs' meaning-making resources. Mrs. Dixon is focusing on the phase of "Building Shared Knowledge" through Detailed Reading and examining how the textbook is *presenting content*. Specifically, she is exploring the language of the text with students by discussing the use of the process *are covered* in the text. Mrs. Dixon calls students' attention to this pattern and asks them to notice why *covered* is not used in other examples when the text discussed *hair or fur*. This part of the text was "All mammals have hair or fur." This is part of a collaborative activity in which students were engaged and discussed challenging concepts. Mrs. Dixon asked Alena, a ML, a specific question, drawing on her linguistic resources. After this "language dissection," students played a game and continued to explore the language of the text. Mrs. Dixon explained in her lesson plan that she selected this text because it presented key concepts about animals and their classification, including their bodies.

Choosing a particular text and deconstructing its language features is a critical component of a functional approach and provides more than an abstract focus on language. MLs have opportunities to explore the different patterns of language that construct different types of texts (see de Oliveira, 2016, for a full discussion). By focusing on texts, Mrs. Dixon was able to highlight key language patterns that present specific content, which encourages conversation in the classroom about which content is presented, who is represented and how, and how the text is organized.

Mrs. Dixon was able to show her MLs how language works in science, a practice that highlights how language expresses disciplinary knowledge. In order to develop lessons, Mrs. Dixon began with the selection of key concepts then designed units of study that incorporated language analysis based on a functional approach to highlight the key concepts in her content curriculum. She chose a related text and developed a guiding question that focused on language analysis and discussion. Then she engaged in language analysis using a functional approach, first to learn more about the text herself, and then to design activities that could engage her MLs in seeing the multiple meanings embedded in the text. As the example presented shows, teachers can develop ways to talk about both language and content in ways that help MLs access the language of the text so they can understand the content better.

The next example comes from the first-grade classroom with Ms. Cabana. The content area was English language arts/literacy. The lesson is centered around the Joint Construction phase of the TLC in which the teacher shares responsibility with students for writing the same genre and co-constructs another example of this genre based on suggestions from students (see de Oliveira, Jones, & Smith, 2021, for a full description). The teacher is typically in front of the room *scribing* while everyone is *writing* together. The Building Shared Knowledge through Detailed Reading phase focused on exploring how the text is written and how it accomplishes its goals through its language choices. Notes were displayed on the board via projector so that students and teacher had a common vocabulary and set of grammatical structures (common phrasings unique to the genre) from which to draw. The specific lesson is based on the book *Last Stop on Market Street* (de la Peña, 2015).

Last Stop on Market Street (de la Peña, 2015) is about a boy named CJ riding the bus with his grandma. CJ asks several questions, which are answered in an inspiring way by grandma, who helps him appreciate the world around them. Ms. Cabana planned several interactions that drew upon the different parts of Detailed Reading to engage students in discussions about the book. A major part of the TLC is a shared experience, and Ms. Cabana brainstormed with students ways that they could help the community, as CJ, the main character, helped at the soup kitchen with his grandma. The students voted and decided that they would collect food items to make Thanksgiving baskets for the "Feed South Florida" initiative, which provides food and other resources to those who need it. Students brought in their own donations and solicited donations from other students and staff members at the school. Because the TLC is based on the principle "guidance through interaction in the context of shared experiences," Ms. Cabana thought about using this shared experience as a springboard for writing.

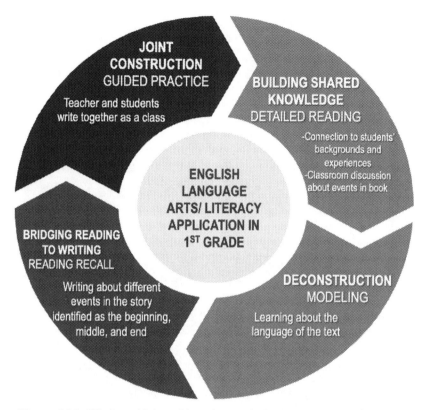

Figure 6 Modified teaching and learning cycle for Ms. Cabana's first-grade classroom

Another important part of the TLC is the Deconstruction phase in which the teacher deconstructs a mentor text with students. For this lesson, we collaboratively constructed a mentor text that captured the major events of the *Last Stop.* Ms. Cabana displayed the mentor text on the board and used it to discuss different aspects including language used, topic sentence, common and proper nouns, and transitions. Ms. Cabana felt like she needed to add an additional phase to the TLC because her first-grade students needed additional practice that bridged the reading and writing components (see Figure 6). She, therefore, added a phase to the TLC that we call *Bridging Reading and Writing* so first graders would be more prepared for the other phases of the TLC. Ms. Cabana had the following content and language objectives and used the following materials:

Content Objectives: Students will be able to identify central themes and main events from *Last Stop on Market Street.*

Language Objectives: Students will be able to write a narrative recount based on the steps they completed during their shared experience of collecting and distributing food for the "Feed South Florida" initiative.

Materials: *Last Stop on Market Street* book, smart board and/or overhead projector, *Last Stop on Market Street* mentor text (for purposes of deconstruction), graphic organizer (for joint construction planning).

Desired Outcomes: After completion of this lesson, students will have the ability to identify central themes and main events in narratives. Students will also be able to write narrative recounts.

Ms. Cabana began the lesson by asking students, "First of all, has anyone gone away to visit a family member?" This question initiates discussion in which students share their experiences of visiting their grandparents, cousins, aunts/uncles, and so on.

Building Shared Knowledge: Detailed Reading, *Last Stop on Market Street*

Ms. Cabana engaged the students in a conversation about the front cover of the book. She asked students to make predictions about the content of the book based on the illustration(s) they saw.

Excerpt 6

Ms. Cabana: I want everyone to look at the cover of *Last Stop on Market Street* and I want you to notice all the details you see in this cover. I want you to think "what is going on in this picture?" Now I want you to turn to someone who is near you and tell them what you think is going on in this picture.

Ms. Cabana engaged students in a discussion of the front cover and then told students to conduct a picture walk of the book. She stated, "You are just looking at the illustrations and seeing if you can guess what is happening." Ms. Cabana then told students that she would read the entire book to them without stopping. She encouraged them to save their questions for the end. After reading the entire book, Ms. Cabana invited students to share their observations and perceptions about the story with their classmates. Students brought up ideas about the characters in the story, the relationship between the two main characters (CJ and Nana), and the way the town looks in the illustrations. Ms. Cabana began to discuss the image/text relationship with students in order to talk about the character's feelings. She encouraged students to pay close attention to both illustrations and text instead of just relying on one or the other. She also related how the character feels with how they might feel at certain times in their own lives.

An example of this was: Ms. Cabana: Boys and girls when you push out of the school doors you are free to do whatever you want. That is how CJ was feeling.

Based on this discussion Ms. Cabana directed students to work together on a graphic organizer to identify the CJ's feelings with evidence from the story about his actions and what he says.

CJ

Action	Says

After completing the graphic organizer with a partner, students were directed by Ms. Cabana to come back together as a class to discuss their findings from the story. Then Ms. Cabana invited students to participate in a discussion about the different parts of the story labeled as, "beginning, middle, end." She informed students that they are identifying the parts of the story so they can write about it the following day. Ms. Cabana wrote the middle part on the board for students to see and think about, "CJ heard the music and it made him happy." She then instructed students to work with a buddy (and their book) to identify the beginning and end parts of the story. She circulated around the room to help pairs of students.

Deconstruction

Ms. Cabana began the deconstruction process by displaying the mentor text on the smart board for everyone to see. The mentor text is below.

> CJ had a busy day on Sunday! First, CJ and Nana went to church. After church, CJ and Nana waited for the bus in the rain. When CJ and Nana got on the bus, they saw many different people. CJ listened to the music played by the guitar player. After the song, CJ dropped a coin in the man's hat. Then, CJ heard the bus driver call for the "last stop on Market Street." Soon after, CJ and Nana stepped off the bus and walked down the sidewalk. CJ noticed that it was dirty, but then he saw a perfect rainbow over their soup kitchen. Once CJ saw everyone inside he told Nana that he was glad they came.

She began by pointing out whole text features and asking students about the paragraph format and the indent of the first line. She then instructed students to read the text with her out loud. After reading the text, she began to ask students questions about what they liked from the writing. They provided various responses such as "the rainbow" and "the coin in the man's hat."

Ms. Cabana then started to point out features of the writing that she believed were important. One of the first items was about the topic sentence. Ms. Cabana then moved forward to point out the transitional words used in the mentor text. She asked students to point out the different transitional words they notice in the mentor text. As they identified the transitional words she asked students to highlight them on the smart board for everyone to see. Ms. Cabana then asked students to think of other words they might use in their own writing to transition from one event to the next. She wrote their ideas on the smart board next to the mentor text. Ms. Cabana then led a discussion to review what students learned about "good writing" through the deconstruction process. She encouraged students to think of ways they can use these good writing strategies in their own writing. Ms. Cabana returned to the mentor text to review the use of common and proper nouns. She instructed students to read through the entire text with her and then asked for volunteers to highlight the proper and common nouns they saw in the text.

Bridging Reading to Writing

After going through the deconstruction process, Ms. Cabana directed students to take their planning sheet that they had completed a few days prior and begin their writing about the different events in the story identified as the beginning, middle, and end. Ms. Cabana asked for volunteers to share their final written product with the classmates. During this sharing period, students and Ms. Cabana provided feedback to the student sharing their writing by (1) saying something you liked, (2) asking one question, and (3) offering one suggestion to improve the writing.

Joint Construction

Ms. Cabana worked with students to brainstorm ways to help the community (their shared experience) that would influence their joint construction writing piece. As students contributed ideas, Ms. Cabana wrote the ideas on the board in a web organizer. Ms. Cabana and students decide to collect food to make Thanksgiving baskets for people in the community that may not have any. She and the students came up with an advertisement to use to make posters to place around the school to get other students and teachers to donate food for the baskets.

After collecting items and preparing the baskets, Ms. Cabana told the students that they needed to write a letter together (joint construction) to their principal to let her know about what they had been doing for their community. Ms. Cabana typed on the smart board for all students to see and instructed them to scribe while she types. The first step was to plan for the writing so she and the students drew three boxes to write the three main things they did for their community project. Ms. Cabana asked students to volunteer to talk about the things they did for the project. She helped them put their thoughts into sentences and placed emphasis on transitional words that they had been learning throughout the lesson. The next step in the joint construction process was for Ms. Cabana and the students to write their letter to the principal (based on the plan they wrote the previous day). Ms. Cabana talked with students to get their input about the best way to write their letter. Ms. Cabana and the students decided on each piece of the letter together and the students wrote their own letters as Ms. Cabana typed for them to see on the smart board. Ms. Cabana and the students delivered the letters to the principal.

4 Implications for Teacher Education

This Element highlights five culturally sustaining teaching practices for young MLs with concrete examples from several elementary classrooms. We intentionally bring into focus practices that embody culturally sustaining pedagogies which enable educators to create learning environments in which all students are educated effectively and equitably. This focus on culturally sustaining pedagogies is particularly important for MLs who are often overlooked in general education classrooms (Lucas & Villegas, 2011). As such, this work holds multiple implications for a number of stakeholders, including teachers, practitioners, teacher educators, and scholars. These practices may unfold differently based on varied instructional contexts, but all educators must be prepared to incorporate these practices in support of their MLs. They affirm students' experiences, language backgrounds, and linguistic repertoires while striving to expand them, not as part of a hegemonic notion that a discourse is more important or relevant than others but to emphasize meaning making as a contextual process connected to various situations.

The five practices presented in this Element can be used to address the multifaceted needs of MLs. From a sociocultural perspective, teachers should affirm and expand on MLs' prior knowledge and language practices. In order to do this, teachers will need to carefully plan and purposefully incorporate particular teaching strategies to draw on their students' diverse funds of knowledge which are often overlooked (e.g., Gee, 1996; Gonzalez et al., 2005). A large portion of this work will stem from teachers getting to know their students so they can leverage that knowledge in the classroom. There are many approaches that teachers can utilize here, but research has pointed specifically to resources such as literacy profiles, "all about me" projects (e.g., family biography, informational poster), questionnaires/surveys, and communication with families (Herrera et al., 2015; Short et al., 2018). The information gathered through these resources can help teachers build a comprehensive understanding of their MLs' social, cultural, and emotional assets which will allow them to better support their learning and growth.

From an academic perspective, teachers need knowledge and practical ideas related to facilitating MLs' content and ongoing English language development simultaneously. Drawing on the five practices presented here allows teachers to provide MLs with the access they need to learn content and language while supporting and expanding their cultural and linguistic competencies. One way to bring the varied practices together in an instructional way is to build lessons or units that implement a functional approach to language development, enacted with the TLC at the center. The TLC affords teachers flexibility when it comes to selecting which phases will be implemented in their classroom. For example, the teacher may elect to focus solely on the deconstruction and joint construction phases for a couple iterations in order to provide students with additional scaffolding before releasing responsibility to them in a collaborative or individual activity. Alternatively, a teacher may notice that the students are ready to write independently right away and may choose to skip the collaborative construction phase. The TLC offers multiple avenues for students to engage with complex tasks, both as readers and writers. Creating lessons with this pedagogical tool allows students to gradually become more independent and responsible for their own language and literacy development. We outline practical steps for implementing the TLC in the classroom here:

1. *Identify a mentor text* that aligns with the target genre, curriculum standards and objectives, and student needs. Ideally the selection would be a culturally relevant text that gives the teacher multiple opportunities to connect to students' L1s and cultures, utilize translanguaging, and draw on students' diverse funds of knowledge.

2. *Conduct an analysis of the text and select the language features* that students will want to focus on within the mentor text and identify relevant content to build shared knowledge. Use multimodal instruction to build shared knowledge.

3. *Conduct a Detailed Reading and deconstruction of the mentor text* by first discussing the purpose, text structures, and language features typical of that genre. Following this discussion, the teacher provides explicit instruction and modeling to identify the content and organization of the text. Oftentimes the teacher leads whole-class discussions through mini-lesson(s) which allows for

a focus on different aspects of the text. The teacher can highlight or underline the text's key language features on a whiteboard or interactive board.

4. *Jointly construct a class text from the focal genre* based on a shared experience. During this phase, the teacher acts as a scribe and solicits students' input to craft the text, drawing on various scaffolding moves (e.g., cueing, recasting) to bridge the everyday language students are accustomed to using for social purposes with the academic language appropriate for the text in the new genre (de Oliveira, 2017). Importantly, the teacher instructs students to use the deconstructed text as a model, drawing their attention to the purpose, stages, and language features of the genre.

5. *Release students to collaboratively produce a text with a partner or small group of peers.* The teacher encourages students to reference both the deconstructed and jointly constructed texts as they craft their own text in the new genre.

6. *Direct students to independently construct their own texts.* Students write independently, with teacher support as needed.

With the enactment of a functional approach through the TLC, teachers can implement all of the culturally sustaining teaching practices described in this Element.

4.1 Teacher Preparation for Culturally Sustaining Practices

Teacher education programs play a vital role in preparing teachers to work with MLs. We argue that their coursework and practicum experiences centered on elements of diversity, equity, and inclusion should also incorporate a focus on the five practices identified in this Element. In fact, these five practices should be embedded in the curriculum of all teacher preparation programs so that all content area teachers, bilingual specialists, ESOL specialists, and special education teachers have the knowledge and experience to apply these practices in their future classrooms.

While we show the importance of teachers' use of students' home language in the classroom, it is critical that teacher education programs include experiences that teach practical strategies for effectively incorporating L1 use in instruction. As teachers continue to develop this understanding, they also need to develop expertise in scaffolding. Scaffolding is a complex process that involves several elements that can be brought to further attention. Expertise in interactional scaffolding, in particular, should be a focus of attention as opportunities for MLs to interact in the classroom with teachers and students are vital for their language development. We advocate for integration of multimodal instruction into teacher education programs to better prepare teachers for an expanded view of language development that encompasses use of multiple modes including image, writing, gesture, gaze, speech, and posture, as well as multisensory elements for meaning making across content areas.

The examples presented in this Element come from a variety of primary grade levels and contexts underscoring that this work has the potential to be effective in all settings. We suggest that teacher education programs select diverse school sites for pre-service teachers' practicum experiences and incorporate corresponding assignments specifically focused on these practices (e.g., journal entries, case reports, interviews).

4.2 Future Research Directions

There are a number of pathways forward with this important work that can continue to shed light on the benefits and challenges of incorporating culturally sustaining practices with MLs. One opportunity lies in integrating these practices with other core practices for working with multilingual students, including knowing students, building a positive learning environment, planning and enacting content and language instruction that meets the needs of MLs, and supporting students' language and literacy development (Peercy et al., 2022; Peercy & Chi, 2022).

An additional area for further work centers around pre-service teachers and their development as culturally sustaining educators. With teacher preparation programs embedding these practices in the curriculum, more research is needed that focuses on how pre-service teachers understand and apply these practices in their coursework and internship. As teachers across content areas work with MLs, this research would focus on pre-service teachers enrolled in various teacher preparation programs (e.g., elementary education, secondary education, ESOL, special education). In addition, the work on culturally sustaining teaching practices should also be incorporated into professional learning opportunities for in-service teachers who already work or will have this population of students in their classes. This work should include professional learning spaces where in-service teachers of all content areas are working to develop new teaching practices for elementary and secondary classrooms. We hope to see more studies that focus on MLs' resources and how they draw on their cultural and linguistic affordances to learn new ways of making meaning in different content areas – English language arts, mathematics, and social studies, in particular. In addition, future work should focus on teacher educators' efforts to infuse these practices into their teacher education classes to show their power and possibilities.

We also would like to conclude with a call for studies that are designed to assess the relative effectiveness of the approaches recommended in this

Element. Studies using various methodological approaches including quantitative and qualitative. Specifically, experimental research may support stronger claims about effectiveness and to assess whether the theories posited stand up to proper scrutiny.

Furthermore, the examples of classroom-based research put forth here focus on various grades at the elementary level. It would be beneficial for future studies to focus on incorporating culturally sustaining practices in secondary settings. Additionally, it would be helpful to investigate how teachers of all grade levels perceive these practices and the steps they take to incorporate them in their instruction on a daily basis.

We hope the ideas presented in this Element are used in teacher education programs and professional learning settings. Culturally sustaining teaching practices such as the ones we highlight here have much promise in the teaching and learning of young MLs. We are excited to move this conversation forward in the field.

References

Ajayi, L. (2009). English as a second language learners' exploration of multi-modal texts in a junior high school. *Journal of Adolescent & Adult Literacy*, *52*(7), 585–595.

Athanases, S. Z., & de Oliveira, L. C. (2014). Scaffolding versus routine support for Latina/o youth in an urban school: Tensions in building toward disciplinary literacy. *Journal of Literacy Research*, *46*(2), 263–299.

Bean, J., Eddy, R., Grego, R. et al. (2003). Should we invite students to write in home languages? Complicating the yes/no debate. *Composition Studies*, *31*(1), 25–42.

Blair, A., Haneda, M., & Bose, F. N. (2018). Reimagining English-medium instructional settings as sites of multilingual and multimodal meaning making. *TESOL Quarterly*, *52*(3), 516–539.

Bland, J. (Ed.). (2015). *Teaching English to young learners: Critical issues in language teaching with 3–12 year old*s. Bloomsbury.

Brisk, M. E. (2015). *Engaging students in academic literacies: Genre-based pedagogy for K-5 classrooms*. Routledge.

Brisk, M. E., Hodgson-Drysdale, T., & O'Connor, C. (2011). A study of a collaborative instructional project informed by systemic functional linguistic theory: Report writing in elementary grades. *Journal of Education*, *191*(1), 1–12.

Brisk, M. E., & Zisselsberger, M. (2011). "We've let them in on the secret": Using SFL theory to improve the teaching of writing to bilingual learners. In T. Lucas (Ed.), *Teacher preparation for linguistically diverse classrooms: A resource for teacher educators* (pp. 111–126). Routledge.

Bruner, J. (1983). *Child's talk: Learning to use language*. Norton.

Caplan, N. A., & Farling, M. (2017). A dozen heads are better than one: Collaborative writing in genre-based pedagogy. *TESOL Journal*, *8*(3), 564–581.

Cenoz, J., & Gorter, D. (2021). *Pedagogical translanguaging*. Cambridge University Press. DOI: 10.1017/9781009029384.

Chung, Y. H., & Walsh, D. J. (2006). Constructing a joint story-writing space: The dynamics of young children's collaboration at computers. *Early Education and Development*, *17*(3), 373–420.

Clark, D. (2022). Percentage of pupils whose first language is not English in England 2015–2021. www.statista.com/statistics/330782/england-english-additional-language-primary-pupils/.

Cook, G. (2007). A thing of the future: Translation in language learning. *International Journal of Applied Linguistics, 17*(3), 396–401.

Cook, V. (2001). Using the first language in the classroom. *Canadian Modern Language Review, 57*(3), 402–423.

Creswell, J. W., & Poth, C. N. (2018). *Qualitative inquiry and research design choosing among five approaches* (4th ed.). Sage.

Cummins, J. (2001). Empowering minority students: A framework for intervention. *Harvard Educational Review, 71*(4), 649–676.

Cummins, J. (2005). A proposal for action: Strategies for recognizing heritage language competence as a learning resource within the mainstream classroom. *Modern Language Journal, 89*(4), 585–592.

Cummins, J. (2007). Rethinking monolingual instructional strategies in multilingual classrooms. *Canadian Journal of Applied Linguistics, 10*(2), 221–240.

Cunningham, T. H., & Graham, C. (2000). Increasing native English vocabulary recognition through Spanish immersion: Cognate transfer from foreign to first language. *Journal of Educational Psychology, 92*(1), 37–49.

de Jong, E. J., Harper, C. A., & Coady, M. R. (2013). Enhanced knowledge and skills for elementary mainstream teachers of English language learners. *Theory into Practice, 52*(2), 89–97.

de la Peña, M. (2015). *Last stop on Market Street*. Penguin Books.

de Oliveira, L. C. (2016). A language-based approach to content instruction (LACI) for English language learners: Examples from two elementary teachers. *International Multilingual Research Journal, 10*(3), 217–231.

de Oliveira, L. C. (2017). A genre-based approach to L2 writing instruction in K-12. *TESOL Connections*. http://newsmanager.commpartners.com/tesolc/downloads/features/2017/2017-07-TLC.pdf.

de Oliveira, L. C., & Athanases, S. Z. (2017). A framework to reenvision instructional scaffolding for linguistically diverse learners. *Journal of Adolescent & Adult Literacy, 61*(2), 123–129.

de Oliveira, L. C., Gilmetdinova, A., & Pelaez-Morales, C. (2015). The use of Spanish by a monolingual kindergarten teacher to support English language learners. *Language and Education, 29*(6), 1–21.

de Oliveira, L. C., Jones, L., & Smith, S. L. (2020). Interactional scaffolding in a first-grade classroom through the teaching–learning cycle. *International Journal of Bilingual Education and Bilingualism*, 1–19. DOI: 10.1080/13670050.2020.1798867.

de Oliveira, L. C., Jones, L., & Smith, S. L. (2021). A language-based approach to content instruction (LACI) for multilingual learners: Six Cs of scaffolding in first grade. *Journal of Language, Identity, and Education*. DOI: 10.1080/15348458.2021.1885409.

de Oliveira, L. C., Klassen, M., & Maune, M. (2015). From detailed reading to independent writing: Scaffolding instruction for ELLs through knowledge about language. *The Common Core State Standards in English Language Arts for English Language Learners: Grades, 6–12*. TESOL Press.

de Oliveira, L. C., & Lan, S. W. (2014). Writing science in an upper elementary classroom: A genre-based approach to teaching English language learners. *Journal of Second Language Writing*, *25*, 23–39.

de Oliveira, L. C., & Westerlund, R. (2021). A functional approach to language development for dual language learners. *Journal of English Learner Education*, *12*(1), 1–23.

Derewianka, B., & Jones, P. (2016). *Teaching language in context*. Oxford University Press.

Edstrom, A. (2006). L1 use in the L2 classroom: One teacher's self-evaluation. *Canadian Modern Language Review*, *63*(2), 275–292.

Faltis, C., Arias, M. B., & Ramírez-Marín, F. (2010). Identifying relevant competencies for secondary teachers of English learners. *Bilingual Research Journal*, *33*(3), 307–328. doi:10.1080/15235882.2010.52935.

Fang, Z. & Schleppegrell, M. (2008). *Reading in secondary content areas: A language-based pedagogy*. University of Michigan Press.

Fleming, N. D., & Mills, C. (1992). Helping students understand how they learn. *The Teaching Professor*, *7*(4), 44–63.

Flores, N., & Rosa, J. (2015). Undoing appropriateness: Raciolinguistic ideologies and language diversity in education. *Harvard Educational Review*, *85*(2), 149–171.

Gallo, S. (2014). The effects of gendered immigration enforcement on middle childhood and schooling. *American Educational Research Journal*, *51*(3), 473–504.

García, O. (2020). The education of Latinx bilingual children in times of isolation: Unlearning and relearning. *MinneTESOL Journal*, *36*(1). http://minnetesoljournal.org/wp-content/uploads/2020/05/Garci%CC%81a_The-education-of-Latinx-bilingual-children-in-times-of-isolation_-Unlearning-and-relearning.pdf.

García, O., & Kleyn, T. (2013). Teacher education for multilingual education. In C. A. Chapelle (Ed.), *The Encyclopedia of applied linguistics* (pp. 1-6). Blackwell Publishing.

García, O., & Kleyn, T. (Eds.) (2016). *Translanguaging with multilingual students: Learning from classroom moments*. Routledge.

García, E., & Jensen, B. (2009). Early educational opportunities for children of Hispanic origins. *Social Policy Report*, *23*(2), 1–19.

García, O., & Li, W. (2014). *Translanguaging: Language, bilingualism and education*. Palgrave Macmillan.

Gebhard, M. (2019). *Teaching and researching ELLs' disciplinary literacies: Systemic functional linguistics in action in the context of U.S. school reform*. Routledge.

Garton, S., & Copland, F. (Eds.) (2019). *Routledge handbook of teaching English to young learners*. Routledge.

Gebhard, M., Harman, R., & Seger, W. (2007). Reclaiming recess: Learning the language of persuasion. *Language Arts, 84*(5), 419–430.

Gee, J. (1996). *Social linguistics and literacies: Ideology in discourses*. Routledge.

Gibbons, P. (2006). *Bridging discourses in the ESL classroom: Students, teachers and researchers*. A&C Black.

Gibbons, P. (2015). *Scaffolding language, scaffolding learning: Teaching English language learners in the mainstream classroom* (2nd ed.). Heinemann.

Gonzalez, N., Moll, L. C., & Amanti, C. (2005). *Funds of knowledge: Theorizing practices in households, communities, and classrooms*. Routledge.

Gort, M., & Pontier, R. W. (2013). Exploring bilingual pedagogies in dual language preschool classrooms. *Language and Education, 27*(3), 223–245.

Gunderson, L. (2009). *ESL(ELL) literacy instruction: A guidebook to theory and practice* (2nd ed.). Routledge.

Gutiérrez, K. D., Sengupta-Irving, T., & Dieckmann, J. (2010). Developing a mathematical vision: Mathematics as a discursive and embodied practice. In J. Moschkovich (Ed.), *Language and mathematics education: Multiple perspectives and directions for research* (pp. 29–71). Information Age Publishing.

Halliday, M. A. K., & Matthiessen, C. M. I. M. (2014). *Halliday's introduction to functional grammar* (4th ed.). Routledge.

Hammond, J., & Gibbons, P. (2005). Putting scaffolding to work: The contribution of scaffolding in articulating ESL education. *Prospect, 20*(1), 6–30.

Harrison, D. L. (2001). *Johnny Appleseed: My story*. Random House.

Harman, R. (2013). Literary intertextuality in genre-based pedagogies: Building lexical cohesion in fifth-grade L2 writing. *Journal of Second Language Writing, 22*(2), 125–140. DOI: 10.1016/j.jslw.2013.03.006.

Harman, R., & Khote, N. (2017). Critical SFL praxis with bilingual youth: Disciplinary instruction in a third space. *Critical Inquiry in Language Studies, 2*, 1–21. https://doi.org/10.1080/15427587.2017.1318663.

Hedges, H., Cullen, J., & Jordan, B. (2011). Early years curriculum: Funds of knowledge as a conceptual framework for children's interests. *Journal of Curriculum Studies, 43*(2), 185–205.

Herrera, S. G., Perez, D. R., & Escamilla, K. (2015). *Teaching reading to English language learners: Differentiated literacies* (2nd ed.). Allyn & Bacon/Pearson.

Hite, C. E., & Evans, L. S. (2006). Mainstream first-grade teachers' understanding of strategies for accommodating the needs of English language learners. *Teacher Education Quarterly, 33*(2), 89–110.

Hogg, L. (2011). Funds of knowledge: An investigation of coherence within the literature. *Teaching and Teacher Education, 27*(3), 666–677.

Howard, T. C., & Aleman, G. R. (2008). Teacher capacity for diverse learners: What do teachers need to know. In M. Cochran-Smith, S. Feiman- Nemser, D. J. McIntyre, & K. E. Demers (Eds.), *Handbook of research on teacher education: Enduring questions in changing contexts* (pp. 157–174). Routledge.

Hyland, K. (2007). Genre pedagogy: Language, literacy and L2 writing instruction. *Journal of Second Language Writing, 16*(3), 148–164.

Jewitt, C. (2005). Technology, literacy and learning: A multimodal approach. Routledge.

Jewitt, C. (Ed.). (2009). *The Routledge handbook of multimodal analysis.* Routledge.

Johnson, E. M. (2019). Choosing and using interactional scaffolds: How teachers' moment-to-moment supports can generate and sustain emergent bilinguals' engagement with challenging English texts. *Research in the Teaching of English, 53*(3), 245–269.

Johnston, P. H. (2012). *Opening minds: Using language to change lives.* Stenhouse.

Keefer, N., Lopez, J., Young, J., & Haj-Broussard, M. (2020). Gathering funds of knowledge: An elementary social studies unit plan for bilingual settings. *Social Studies and the Young Learner, 33*(2), 14–19.

Kerfoot, C., & Van Heerden, M. (2015). Testing the waters: Exploring the teaching of genres in a Cape Flats Primary School in South Africa. *Language and Education, 29*(3), 235–255.

Khote, N. (2018). Translanguaging in systemic functional linguistics: A culturally sustaining pedagogy for writing in secondary schools. In R. Harman (Ed.), *Bilingual learners and social equity* (pp. 153–178). Springer.

Kress, G., Ogborn, J., Jewitt, C., & Tsatsarelis, C. (2001). *The rhetorics of the science classroom: A multimodal approach.* Economic and Social Research Council.

Ladson-Billings, G. (2014). Culturally relevant pedagogy 2.0: Aka the remix. *Harvard Educational Review, 84*(1), 74–84.

Lenters, K., & Winters, K. L. (2013). Fracturing writing spaces: Multimodal storytelling ignites process writing. *The Reading Teacher, 67*(3), 227–237.

Llopart, M., & Esteban-Guitart, M. (2018). Funds of knowledge in 21st century societies: Inclusive educational practices for under-represented students. A literature review. *Journal of Curriculum Studies, 50*(2), 145–161.

Lotherington, H., & Jenson, J. (2011). Teaching multimodal and digital literacy in L2 settings: New literacies, new basics, new pedagogies. *Annual Review of Applied Linguistics, 31*, 226–246.

Lucas, T., & Villegas, A. M. (2011). A framework for preparing linguistically responsive teachers. In T. Lucas (Ed.), *Teacher preparation for linguistically diverse classrooms: A resource for teacher educators* (pp. 55–72). Routledge.

Martin, J. R. (2009). Genre and language learning: A social semiotic perspective. *Linguistics and Education, 20*(1), 10–21.

Martin, J. R., & Rose, D. (2005). Designing literacy pedagogy: Scaffolding democracy in the classroom. *Continuing discourse on language: A functional perspective, 1*, 251–280.

Martínez, R. A., Orellana, M. F., Pacheco, M., & Carbone, P. (2008). Found in translation: Connecting translating experiences to academic writing. *Language Arts, 85*(6), 421–431.

Mead, J. (2021). Teachers' experiences incorporating English language learners' funds of knowledge into scripted curricula. Unpublished Dissertation, Georgia State University. https://scholarworks.gsu.edu/mse_diss/104.

Mehan, H. (1979). 'What time is it, Denise?" Asking known information questions in classroom discourse. *Theory into Practice, 18*(4), 285–294.

Michell, M (2021). How many English as an additional language or dialect (EAL/D) learners are there in Australian schools? https://tesol.org.au/how-many-english-as-an-additional-language-or-dialect-eal-d-learners-are-there-in-australian-schools/.

Moje, E. B., Ciechanowski, K. M., Kramer, K. et al. (2004). Working toward third space in content area literacy: An examination of everyday funds of knowledge and discourse. *Reading Research Quarterly, 39*(1), 38–70.

Moll, L., Amanti, C., Neff, D., & Gonzalez, N. (1992). Funds of knowledge for teaching: Using a qualitative approach to connect homes and classrooms. *Theory into Practice, 31*(2), 132–141. DOI: 10.1080/0040584920 9543534.

Moore, J., & Schleppegrell, M. (2014). Using a functional linguistics metalanguage to support academic language development in the English Language Arts. *Linguistics and Education, 26*, 92–105.

Morales, J., Schissel, J. L., & López-Gopar, M. (2020). Pedagogical sismo: Translanguaging approaches for English language instruction and assessment in Oaxaca, Mexico. In Z. Tian, L. Aghai, P. Sayer, & J. L. Schissel (Eds)., *Envisioning TESOL through a translanguaging lens: Global perspectives* (pp. 161–183). Springer.

NCES (National Center for Education Statistics). (2020). English language learners in public schools. https://nces.ed.gov/programs/coe/indicator_cgf .asp.

Ortega, L. (2013). Ways forward for a bi/multilingual turn in SLA. In S. May (Ed.), *The multilingual turn: Implications for SLA, TESOL, and bilingual education* (pp. 32–52). Routledge.

Pacheco, M. B., & Smith, B. E. (2015). Across languages, modes, and identities: Bilingual adolescents' multimodal codemeshing in the literacy classroom. *Bilingual Research Journal, 38*(3), 292–312.

Palincsar, A. S., & Schleppegrell, M. J. (2014). Focusing on language and meaning while learning with text. *TESOL Quarterly, 48*(3), 616–623.

Pappas, C. C., Varelas, M., Gill, S., Ortiz, I., & Keblawe-Shamah, N. (2009). Research directions: Multimodal books in science-literacy units: Language and visual images for meaning making. *Language Arts, 86*(3), 201–211.

Paris, D. (2012). Culturally sustaining pedagogy: A needed change in stance, terminology, and practice. *Educational Researcher, 41*(3), 93–97.

Paris, D., & Alim, H. S. (Eds.). (2017). *Culturally sustaining pedagogies: Teaching and learning for justice in a changing world.* Teachers College Press.

Peercy, M. M., Tigert, J., Fredricks,D. et al. (2022). From humanizing principles to humanizing practices: Exploring core practices as a bridge to enacting humanizing pedagogy with multilingual students. *Teaching and Teacher Education, 113*, 1–14.

Peercy, M. M., & Chi, J. (2022). "Oh, I was scaffolding!" Novice teachers learning to teach multilingual youth. In L. C. de Oliveira, & R. Westerlund (Eds.), *Scaffolding for multilingual learners in elementary and secondary schools* (pp. 102–120) Routledge.

Polio, C. G., & Duff, P. A. (1994). Teachers' language use in university foreign language classrooms: A qualitative analysis of English and target language alternation. *The Modern Language Journal, 78*(3), 313–326.

Poza, L. (2017). Translanguaging: Definitions, implications, and further needs in burgeoning inquiry. *Berkeley Review of Education, 6*, 101–128.

Ramos, F. (2005). Spanish teachers' opinions about the use of Spanish in mainstream English classrooms before and after their first year in California. *Bilingual Research Journal, 29*(2), 411–433.

Reyes, I. (2012). Biliteracy among children and youths. *Reading Research Quarterly, 47*(3), 307–327.

Rodriguez, G. M. (2013). Power and agency in education: Exploring the pedagogical dimensions of funds of knowledge. *Review of Research in Education, 37*(1), 87–120.

Rolin-Ianziti, J., & Varshney, R. (2008). Students' views regarding the use of the first language: An exploratory study in a tertiary context maximizing target language use. *Canadian Modern Language Review, 65*(2), 249–273.

Rose, D., & Martin, J. R. (2012). *Learning to write, reading to learn: Genre, knowledge and pedagogy in the Sydney School*. Equinox.

Schleppegrell, M. J., Achugar, M., & Oteíza, T. (2004). The grammar of history: Enhancing content-based instruction through a functional focus on language. *TESOL Quarterly, 38*(1), 67–93.

Schleppegrell, M. J. (2004). *The language of schooling: A functional linguistics perspective*. Erlbaum.

Schleppegrell, M. J. (2013). Systemic functional linguistics. In J. P. Gee, & M. Handford (Eds.), *The Routledge handbook of discourse analysis* (pp. 47–60). Routledge.

Schleppegrell, M. J. (2020). The knowledge base for language teaching: What is the English to be taught as content? *Language Teaching Research, 24*(1), 17–27.

Schulze, J. (2011). Writing to persuade: A systemic functional view. *GIST Educational and Learning Research Journal 5*(1), 127–157. DOI: 10.26817%2F16925777.78.

Shin, J. K., & Crandall, J. (2013). *Teaching young learners English: From theory to practice*. National Geographic Learning / Heinle, Cengage Learning.

Short, D., Becker, H., Cloud, N., & Hellman, A. B. (2018). *The 6 principles for exemplary teaching of English learners: Grades K-12*. TESOL Press.

Symons, C., & Bian, Y. (2022). Using SFL in linguistically responsive instruction with multilingual youth: A self-study. *International Journal of TESOL Studies, 4*(2), 91–107. DOI: 10.46451/ijts.2022.02.07.

Takeuchi, M. (2015). The situated multiliteracies approach to classroom participation: English language learners' participation in classroom mathematics practices. *Journal of Language, Identity & Education, 14*(3), 159–178.

't Gilde, J., & Volman, M. (2021). Finding and using students' funds of knowledge and identity in superdiverse primary schools: A collaborative action research project. *Cambridge Journal of Education, 51*, 673–692.

Turner, E. E., Aguirre, J., McDuffie, A. R., & Foote, M. Q. (2019). Jumping into modeling: Elementary mathematical modeling with school and community contexts. *North American Chapter of the International Group for the Psychology of Mathematics Education.*

Vygotsky, L.S. (1978). *Mind in society: The development of higher psychological processes.* Harvard University Press.

WIDA. (2020). *WIDA English language development standards framework, 2020 edition: Kindergarten–grade 12.* Board of Regents of the University of Wisconsin System. https://wida.wisc.edu/sites/default/files/resource/WIDA-ELD-Standards-Framework-2020.pdf.

Woo, M. M., Chu, S. K. W., & Li, X. (2013). Peer-feedback and revision process in a wiki mediated collaborative writing. *Educational Technology Research and Development 61*(2), 279–309. DOI: 10.1007/s11423-012-9285-y.

Wood, D., Brunner, J. R., & Ross, G. (1976). The role of tutoring in problem solving. *Journal of Child Psychology and Psychiatry, 17*(2), 89–100. DOI: 10.1111/j.14697610.1976.tb00381.x

Yi, Y., & Choi, J. (2015). Teachers' views of multimodal practices in K-12 classrooms: Voices from teachers in the United States. *TESOL Quarterly, 49*(4), 838–847.

Cambridge Elements ≡

Language Teaching

Heath Rose

Linacre College, University of Oxford

Heath Rose is Professor of Applied Linguistics at the University of Oxford. Before moving into academia, Heath worked as a language teacher in Australia and Japan in both school and university contexts. He is author of numerous books, such as *Introducing Global Englishes*, *The Japanese Writing System*, *Data Collection Research Methods in Applied Linguistics*, and *Global Englishes for Language Teaching*. Heath's research interests are situated within the field of second language teaching, and includes work on Global Englishes, teaching English as an international language, self-regulated learning, and English Medium Instruction.

Jim McKinley

University College London

Jim McKinley is an Associate Professor of Applied Linguistics and TESOL at UCL, Institute of Education, where he serves as Academic Head of Learning and Teaching. His major research areas are second language writing in global contexts, the internationalisation of higher education, and the relationship between teaching and research. Jim has edited or authored numerous books including the *Routledge Handbook of Research Methods in Applied Linguistics*, *Data Collection Research Methods in Applied Linguistics*, and *Doing Research in Applied Linguistics*. He is also an editor of the journal, *System*. Before moving into academia, Jim taught in a range of diverse contexts including the US, Australia, Japan and Uganda.

Advisory Board

Brian Paltridge, *University of Sydney*
Gary Barkhuizen, *University of Auckland*
Marta Gonzalez-Lloret, *University of Hawaii*
Li Wei, *UCL Institute of Education*
Victoria Murphy, *University of Oxford*
Diane Pecorari, *City University of Hong Kong*
Christa Van der *Walt, Stellenbosch University*

About the Series

This Elements series aims to close the gap between researchers and practitioners by allying research with language teaching practices, in its exploration of research-informed teaching, and teaching-informed research. The series builds upon a rich history of pedagogical research in its exploration of new insights within the field of language teaching.

Cambridge Elements ≡

Language Teaching

Elements in the Series

A full series listing is available at: https://www.cambridge.org/ELAT

Printed in the United States
by Baker & Taylor Publisher Services